Dassau
Super Étendard

FRÉDÉRIC LERT

KEY
Books

MODERN MILITARY AIRCRAFT SERIES, VOLUME 5

Front cover image: The Super Étendard became a worldwide celebrity in association with the AM39 Exocet missile (No 13 is seen here with a training round). Amazingly enough, France, which had a long and extensive use of the aircraft in combat as a bomber, never fired a single Exocet in combat. (Frédéric Lert)

Back cover image: This SEM showed what it took to be a naval fighter jet: a roubust landing gear, large flaps and slats, good visibility from the cockpit, and last, but not least, a hook! (Frédéric Lert)

Title page image: Fitted with a Damocles targeting pod, SEM No 13 launched from *Charles de Gaulle* for a training mission in 2005. The SEM was the first aircraft in the French inventory to use this pod. (Frédéric Lert)

Contents page image: Super Étendard Modernisé No 48 cleared the deck after landing during carrier qualifications on *Charles de Gaulle* in 2005. (Frédéric Lert)

Published by Key Books
An imprint of Key Publishing Ltd
PO Box 100
Stamford
Lincs PE19 1XQ

www.keypublishing.com

The right of Frédéric Lert to be identified as the author of this book has been asserted in accordance with the Copyright, Designs and Patents Act 1988 Sections 77 and 78.

Copyright © Frédéric Lert, 2021

ISBN 978 1 80282 033 1

Typeset by SJmagic DESIGN SERVICES, India.

Contents

Chapter 1

A Birth Full of Mystères

The beginning of 1956 saw the birth of Générale Aéronautique Marcel Dassault (GAMD), grouping together, under a single company name, all the aeronautical entities bearing the name of Dassault. GAMD was then working on the Mirages – the first of which had its initial flight on 25 June 1955 and would become the patriarch of a prolific family. The MD550 'Mirage 1' had the grace and apparent fragility of an insect. Later came the famous Mirage III.

Marcel Dassault flying colours

The Étendard, which was still only called the 'Mystère XXII', was also created in 1956. With its smooth skin, small, pointed nose and compact size, the aircraft looked more like a 'racer' than a fighter aircraft. The project had been launched three years earlier at the request of the Armée de l'air (French Air Force), which was looking for a light attack aircraft. Quickly renamed 'Étendard II', the prototype was powered by two Turbomeca Gabizo jet engines, with no more than 1,000kg of thrust per unit. It flew on 23 July 1956, a year after the Mirage I. Presented to the Armée de l'air, it was ultimately not accepted. In parallel with this project, however, GAMD had developed a single-jet version, powered by the British Siddeley Orpheus reactor, in order to participate in a NATO competition specifically requiring this engine. Called 'Étendard VI', this aircraft flew only 24 hours after the Étendard II. The wise Marcel Dassault, who wanted to cover all his bases, also had a second version of the single-engine aircraft developed, this time called 'Étendard IV' and equipped with a French reactor, the Snecma's Atar 101.

These three Étendard models all essentially retained the wing developed for the SMB2, the first French fighter supersonic in horizontal flight, with the addition of powerful high-lift devices. A naval version of the Étendard IV was also planned from the start of the project, considering the necessary arrangements for operating from aircraft carriers (arresting hook, folding wing, beefed-up structure, landing gear, etc). With the Armée de l'air turning down the Étendard II and NATO not retaining the Étendard VI, the Étendard IV was the only design remaining. However, the nimble aircraft caught the eye of the Aéronavale (Aéronautique navale – French naval aviation), which was looking for a new aircraft to equip its two future aircraft carriers: *Clemenceau* and *Foch*. The GAMD design office then officially developed a naval version, called the Étendard IVM (M for Marine), which flew for the first time on 21 May 1958, with Jean-Marie Saget at the controls. The aircraft had a classic formula and was equipped with a retractable in-flight refuelling probe, a great first for a French aircraft! The probe was housed in the nose of the aircraft, which also received an anti-spin keel, a unique feature on a fighter aircraft. A total of 90 production aircraft, including 21 IVP photo-reconnaissance versions, were ordered by the French Navy, with the first prototypes entering service in 1961.

Here comes the SUE…

Less than ten years later, the Aéronavale was already starting to think about the successor to the Étendard IVM. The sea assault mission had not changed, even if several new weapons, such as atomic bombs and anti-ship missiles, justified the search for a more powerful aircraft, equipped with a more sophisticated navigation and attack system. In light of the fighting that was developing in Vietnam, the demands for efficiency were also increasing.

On 28 October 1974, the first Super Etendard prototype was being readied for its first flight from Istres Air Force base. (Dassault Aviation)

The first prototype pictured rolling towards the runway for its first flight. (Dassault Aviation)

The supersonic capacity in horizontal flight, however, was not considered essential. The interception missions, meanwhile, had been exclusively given to the Chance Vought Crusaders purchased in the United States.

Dassault then offered a modernised version of the Étendard IVM, the Super Étendard (SUE). The idea was to relaunch the Étendard production line, while introducing into the airframe, which was at that time only about 15 years old, all possible modernisations in three essential areas: avionics, engine and aerodynamics. The French Navy was keen on this solution, but they suggested powering the new aircraft with the American PW J-52 reactor, which also equipped the Skyhawk II. The combination was considered, before ultimately being rejected by the French government. The Super Étendard was powered by a Snecma Atar 8K50 with 5,000kg of thrust, without afterburner. The Super Étendard did not show any pretension at high speeds. The aircraft was even considered 'slow', and, if it reached 480kt at low altitude, it

Above: SUE 01 pictured during its first flight above southern France on 28 October 1974. The aircraft flew supersonic during this flight. (Dassault Aviation)

Left: On 28 October 1974, Jacques Jesberger climbed the ladder for the Super Étendard's first flight. (Dassault Aviation)

was only after a slow acceleration. After considering the various options, the French Navy finally decided on the Super Étendard, to which the green light was definitively given in January 1973.

The idea of a new aircraft is not easy, however. 'A good half of the Marine, if not three quarters, said to themselves that the development of the aircraft was useless, that it was simply a slightly modified Étendard which would not bring much [of] something new', recalled Admiral (retired) Robillard, a former Étendard and Super Étendard pilot. It is true that, in the media at the time, the Super Étendard was sometimes presented as 'an optimised Étendard IV' or even 'a new version of the naval combat aircraft'. 'That was a mistake', insisted Admiral Robillard. 'With a new engine, a new wing and a modern navigation and attack system, it was truly a new aircraft, although the family resemblance was obvious'.

Pictured in March 1975, the second prototype was being readied for its first flight. The nose of the aircraft was modified to carry a laser range finder. (Dassault Aviation)

SUE 01 carried an instrumented pod under the fuselage; it was fitted with high speed cameras to film the load separation. (Dassault Aviation)

With the exception of the navigation and attack system, the initial ambition was to achieve a 90 per cent community level between the two generations of aircraft. In the end, and despite a very similar shape, the Super Étendard was more than 90 per cent new.

The French Navy put in its order on 4 September 1973; it included the production of 60 series aircraft, with an option for two additional batches of 20 aircraft each. The aircraft was scheduled to enter service in 1978.

Once the Super Étendard programme officially launched, things went quickly and well. The French Navy, a small entity used to working in a short loop, was alone on board the programme, without the constraints of any national or international cooperation. The Étendard lineage was another asset, as the expertise of the Dassault company had matured in the field of embarked aircraft. Pilots who worked with both aircraft recalled talking a lot less about hydraulics with the Super Étendard than with its predecessor.

The change to the 'Super' also resulted in three essential improvements:

- the engine: the Atar 8B was changed to the 8K50, which resulted in the gain of 750kg of thrust. This was coupled with the introduction of an auto-throttle.
- the navigation and attack system: the heading indicator and watch was changed to a real weapon system with radar, inertial navigation system (INS) and head-up display (HUD).
- the wing: the new design would give the aircraft excellent performance at low speed. In particular, it was equipped with manually operated slats running the entire length of the leading edge (including the folding section) and double-slotted high-lift flaps on the trailing edge. The result lived up to the expectations of the aerodynamicists since, despite the increased weight of the Super Étendard, the latter lands at a speed of 122kt, around ten knots less than the Étendard IVM. The wing of the Super Étendard, however, retains the general architecture inaugurated on the SMB2, with its characteristic negative dihedral that influences the limitations in the event of crosswinds for operations on land. The wing tip is in fact very close to the runway, particularly when the pilot maintains the nose high for aerodynamic braking. These limitations must be put into perspective in the case of an embarked aircraft, since launching and deck landing are always carried out with a perfectly axed relative wind.

On 23 April 1973, the 1,100-litre fuel tanks were emptied during a trial flight with SUE 01. (Dassault Aviation)

Pictured here was the first embarkment on *Foch* in July 1975. (Dassault Aviation)

The third prototype is seen on the *Foch* catapult, ready for another launch. Note the nose borrowed from an Étendard. (Dassault Aviation)

Above: SUE 01 cleared the deck! Note the bridle falling into the sea. (Dassault Aviation)

Left: Seen here was the first trap on *Clemenceau* for the third prototype, with its characteristic Étendard nose. (Dassault Aviation)

The fact remained that the proposed Super Étendard was cut out for *Foch* and *Clemenceau*: two truly magnificent and successful ships, which were relatively small in size, with the limited length and power of the catapults determining the maximum weight of the aircraft embarked. The Super Étendard, therefore, had to stay within the 12-ton catapult limit, with its 14.30m length and 9.60m wingspan, and with the direct consequence of a modest fuel volume (3,500kg with two external tanks for a consumption of around 40kg per minute).

Admiral Robillard recalled:

With the Crusader, we started out with about 4,350kg internally, with no external fuel tanks. With a fuel flow of about 1,100kg per hour, we could hold out for a long time [...] Coming from Landivisiau [French Britany], we sometimes found ourselves vertical [over] central France to dogfight with the Mirage IIIs coming from bases in eastern France. After a few minutes of combat, the Mirages quickly set off for their base, while we could hold quietly on the area. The American planes were really designed on another scale. Moreover, when we received US Navy pilots in exchange, they were very surprised at the size of the Super Étendard and its little fuel capacity.

This is where the in-flight refuelling probe came in, since the Aéronavale had perfectly integrated the ability for its attack aircraft to be refuelled by one of the aircraft rigged as a tanker, with a Douglas refuelling pod. Thus equipped, a Super Étendard could deliver 1,500kg to two aircraft at the start of a raid, and another one could do the same on the return leg. If the Super Étendard on its own had a range of around 300 nautical miles using external tanks, the figure could easily be doubled by making use of carrier-based tankers. Few aircraft did better at the time.

Prototypes

To save time and reduce the cost of the programme, three Étendard IVMs were borrowed from the flottilles (French Navy attack squadrons) and used as prototypes for the SUE. These were Étendard 68, 18 and 13, which became SUE 01, 02 and 03, respectively. The installation of the Atar 8K50 engine, replacing the less powerful Atar 8B, however, required an enlargement of the inlets in order to feed the engine with the correct volume of air. The fuselage was also widened and adapted to the new Atar.

Above left: Pictured on *Clemenceau*, 03 was about to be catapulted. A Crusader waited for its turn in the background. (Dassault Aviation)

Above right: The 59S escadrille insignia was highly visible on the third prototype's nose. (Dassault Aviation)

Above left: **One more catapult launch for Super Étendard 01 on** *Clemenceau*. **On the nose, the 54S escadrille insignia was already worn out. (Dassault Aviation)**

Above right: **In July 1975, the first prototype was ready on the catapult. Its wings belonged to a former Étendard, identifiable by the lack of slats on the wing tips. (Dassault Aviation)**

The first flight of SUE 01 (ex-Étendard 68) took place on 28 October 1974, in Istres, France. Jacques Jesberger, who had tested the naval version of the Jaguar a few years earlier, was at the controls of the aircraft, which reached 13,200m and Mach 1.18 in a slight nose-down dive. The 01 was subsequently used for engine tuning and flight qualities and performance studies. It accumulated more than 1,100 hours of testing and 50 carrier landings before being decommissioned and used as an instruction tool.

SUE 03 (ex-Étendard 13) was the second to take to the air, on 9 March of the following year. This prototype was the most bizarre, since it married the unchanged fuselage of an Étendard IVM with the new wing of the SUE. For its first flight at the Cazaux air base, it even retained all the markings specific to Étendard IVM 13. These were all features designed to give the aircraft excellent low-speed flight qualities, particularly during landing. Barely 19 days after 03, SUE 02 (ex-Étendard 18) took off for the first time from the Istres base. The aircraft was equipped with a complete navigation and attack system, but it retained the wing of the Étendard IV, easily recognizable by the absence of leading-edge slats on its folding section. SUE 02 participated in the weapon system tests, during which it received a laser range finder. It was also used to evaluate the methods of aligning the onboard INS with that of the aircraft carrier. It subsequently received the Agave radar from Thomson CSF.

In the summer of 1975, the close similarities between the Étendard and Super Étendard allowed an astonishing sleight of hand between the different prototypes. SUE 03, which carried out 90 flights and a complete landing and catapulting campaign on *Clemenceau*, was stripped of its SUE wings. It then reverted to Étendard IVM 13 and returned to its flottille. The orphan wing, which demonstrated all its

Right: Dassault's test pilot, Jacques Jesberger, pictured in front of the second SUE prototype. (Dassault Aviation)

Below: SUE 01 in flight showed its classic, yet elegant silhouette. (Dassault Aviation)

qualities during previous tests, was grafted to SUE 01, which also received the navigation and attack system from SUE 02. At the end of this reconstruction, SUE 01 became the first complete, 100 per cent Super Étendard, and ultimately very close to what the production aircraft would be. Thus 'rigged', the aircraft continued its tests at the Centre d'Expérimentations Pratiques de l'Aéronautique navale (CEPA) in Istres.

Serial manufacturing

The easy development of the aircraft made it possible to launch serial production very quickly, although some testing delays caused the programme to fall a few months behind. These delays had significant financial consequences; in 1974, orders were reduced from 60 firm aircraft with 20 options to only 11 being finally exercised. The total number of aircraft ordered by the French was therefore 71, but an additional 14 were ordered by Argentina. The first production aircraft took off on 24 November 1977 from Bordeaux Mérignac, with Jacques Jesberger once again in command. The production was divided between the various establishments of Dassault and its subcontractors, such as Hurel Dubois and Latécoère. All the elements were then brought to Bordeaux Mérignac, where final assembly and reception flights were carried out. The initial plans showed the manufacture of 22 aircraft in 1978, 35 in 1979, and the last aircraft being distributed between 1980 and 1981. The priority manufacturing of the 14 aircraft intended for Argentina, however, slightly delayed the delivery of the French aircraft, the last of which came off the production line in 1982.

Left: **The production line in Bordeaux Mérignac, in the late 1970s. (Dassault Aviation)**

Below: **Good trap for 01, which was, at the time of photographing, still sporting some calibration painting on the fuselage. (Dassault Aviation)**

What should replace the Étendard?

The replacement of the Étendard IVM by its own descendants was not a given for the French Navy. At the end of the 1960s, it was the embarked version of the Jaguar that seemed most likely to equip aircraft carriers *Foch* and *Clemenceau*. The Jaguar flew for the first time on 14 November 1969, in the hands of Jacques Jesberger. The sea trials conducted in 1970 and 1971 did not, however, give satisfactory results and the programme was abandoned in 1973. The aircraft displayed a crippling defect for the French Navy: it was unable to land on a single engine. It was, therefore, useless since any loss of a reactor on the twin engine required either a diversion or an ejection. A single-engine aircraft, easier and cheaper to use, was the better choice.

As a result, the other three contenders for the Étendard succession were single-engine. The first was a navalised version of the Mirage F1. The future would show that, like the Super Étendard, it had interesting evolutionary potential. It carried more fuel than the SUE and had supersonic performance and an advanced weapon system that would allow it to replace both the Étendard and the Crusader. To decrease landing speed, the project involved increasing the wing area, extending the leading-edge slats and transforming the ailerons into flaperons (mobile surfaces playing both the role of the ailerons and the flaps). The replacement of the 9K50 reactor with an M53, the Mirage 2000's future engine, was also envisaged. Five evaluation flights were carried out at Istres in November 1971, using the Mirage F1-03. Simulated deck landings were carried out and the test pilot, François Champion of the Centre d'Essais en Vol (CEV – test flight centre), did not hide his enthusiasm for the aircraft and its possible navalisation. However, the French Navy did not follow up on this possibility.

The other two contenders came from the United States. They were both already in service on American aircraft carriers and heavily engaged in combat in Vietnam. These were the A4M Skyhawk and the A-7 Corsair II. In September 1972, two Marine A-4Ms accompanied by a KA-3 Skywarrior tanker landed at Landivisiau after a non-stop transatlantic crossing and several air-to-air refuellings.

A Jaguar M pictured landing on *Clemenceau*. Although a twin-engine fighter, the Jaguar did not have enough power to operate safely from the carrier on one engine only. (ARDHAN)

Left: A US Marine Corps A-4M pictured on *Foch* in September 1972. The Vietnam War had recently proved the reliability of this aircraft. (ARDHAN)

Below: Both A-4Ms pictured in front of *Foch*'s island. Even if the aircraft's size was correct for the French carriers, the Skyhawk was seen as an older aircraft, with limited potential for evolution. (ARDHAN)

A Jaguar M seen on *Clemenceau* in 1970. The Jaguar programme would be cancelled in 1973. (ARDHAN)

The aircraft would stay a week on the French naval air base and another one on board *Foch* to be evaluated. The A-4M was a light, versatile and simple aircraft. On the other hand, it was already out of production and represented the end of an evolutionary process, with further development limited. Two possibilities were envisaged – the purchase of second-hand aircraft or the relaunch of the production for French needs only – before being ruled out.

Another serious competitor, the A-7 Corsair II, was put forward in 1972 by the French company SNIAS (which was to become Aerospatiale in 1985), in cooperation with Ling-Temco-Vought. According to the cooperation agreement negotiated on this occasion, 50 per cent of the aircraft would be manufactured in France, with the French also taking care of final assembly in the Saint Nazaire factory. The aircraft was much larger than the other aircraft considered and surprised the Navy with its heavy lift capacity – up to 12 250kg bombs simultaneously! Its radar was considered credible in air-sea mode and the aircraft was capable of receiving a wide range of weapons. However, there were drawbacks to its qualities. The Corsair II was a heavy aircraft (around 20 tons loaded), clumsy and relatively slow when loaded. As the French aircraft carriers were sized to operate the Crusader, the use of the Corsair II could have been possible. However, the limited power of the catapults would not have made the best use of the aircraft's loading capacity. A memorandum presented in 1972 by Aerospatiale specified that the aircraft would be limited to a mass of 15,454kg when catapulted, a far cry from the 19,090kg possible on American aircraft carriers. It would, therefore, be necessary to limit either the fuel load or the bomb load. Deemed too heavy, the Corsair II was logically discarded.

There is no doubt that with some good will, the Skyhawk or Corsair could nevertheless have found their way to *Foch* and *Clemenceau* without too much difficulty, but Marcel Dassault always kept a close eye on the situation, fearing an American solution like the plague. The scenario would repeat itself a quarter of a century later, with the F/A-18 vs Rafale; in 1989, as in 1970, it was out of the question for the French aircraft manufacturer to let the American fox into the French henhouse.

The Super Étendard and its Inertial Navigation System

Unlike the Étendard IV, the Super Étendard benefited from an advanced navigation and attack system, allowing it to use the most modern armaments. These included the Exocet anti-ship missile, developed at the same time as the aircraft, which gave the latter a solid reputation in anti-ship warfare. The SUE was initially equipped with the Agave radar, optimised for sea attack, developed by Electronique Marcel Dassault and produced under the supervision of Thomson CSF. The presence of this radar considerably simplified the problem of returning to the aircraft carrier at the end of the mission. It was a revolution for the French pilots! The aircraft also received a HUD, a mission computer and a Kearfott-Sagem inertial unit (initially similar to the one mounted on the US Navy Corsair II), housed in an electronic bay at the front of the aircraft.

In order to familiarise himself with the use of the inertial power unit, the Super Étendard's programme officer, Lieutenant-Commander Jean-Pierre Robillard, made two flights in a two-seater Harrier equipped with Litton equipment: 'The flights were made on 15 April 1975, from Dunston airfield. The manufacturer pilot, D G Riches, had offered me the front seat, a true mark of confidence. I had then noticed how much interest there could be in having an inertial system. The instrument made it possible to know its position permanently with a rather good accuracy.'

When it entered service, the SUE was the first French combat aircraft equipped with an INS. At a time when the GPS was only a distant dream, the INS equipment allowed autonomous navigation above the vast maritime spaces. The Armée de l'air observed this with a touch of jealousy, perhaps even tinged with bitterness, when the possibility of using the SUE to guide its own aircraft over desert African territories was mentioned.

Thanks to the 'Telemir' connection system, alignment of the inertial system was completed in about ten minutes on the aircraft carrier's deck before the launch. The ship, itself equipped with a bulky and

Above and opposite: The cockpit of the legacy Super Étendard, with the radar hood on the right. (Frédéric Lert)

precise inertial system, transmitted its geographical position to the aircraft. This transmission took place by infrared emission (the receiver was placed at the top of the aircraft's vertical fin), guaranteeing insensitivity to interference and a very high level of discretion; unlike a radio transmission, the infrared emission radiates little and makes interception by the enemy impossible.

Two trial campaigns at sea were run in December 1978 and March 1979. The system proved to be satisfactory, confirming the good reliability and accuracy of the references given by the aircraft carrier.

Once in flight, the inertial unit of the SUE measured the acceleration on the three axes, before deducing by successive mathematical integration the speeds and a geographical position. Provided the aircraft was not shaken too badly, the INS' drift was estimated at around 1.5 nautical miles per hour of flight time. To limit this drift, the pilot would therefore try to reset the INS as often as possible off a remarkable point on the coast.

The introduction of GPS obviously changed the game in navigation. On the latest Super Étendard Modernisé (SEM) Standard, the inertial unit can be reset automatically, every 90 seconds, according to the information provided by the GPS. This adjustment could also be 'forced' by the pilot at any time. Finally, it should be noted that the GPS adjustment did not concern the 'Z track' (the position of the aircraft in the vertical aircraft). This position could, however, be calculated by aiming at a point recognised with the radar, or else with the telemetry function of the laser designation pod.

The muscle of the Super Étendard: the Atar 8K50

Dassault also considered motorising the Super Étendard using an American Pratt & Whitney J52 engine, which powered the Skyhawk II. Although it was appreciated for its power and reliability, he opted for a more local solution with the Atar 8K50 from national engine manufacturer Snecma. This engine was, in fact, a version of the Atar 9K50 that powered the Mirage F1, but without the afterburner. The two engines were so identical that, with the deflation of the Mirage F1 fleet, the Navy was able to recover the 9K50s and convert them into 8K50s for its SEMs by removing the afterburner.

The 8K50 was a nine-stage axial compressor engine with a fixed nozzle and delivered 4,950kg of thrust at sea level. After some initial setbacks, owing to the formation of cracks in the shells, this engine proved its reliability throughout its career. The maximum range of the Super Étendard was determined by the engine's oil consumption, which could reach 1.5 litres per hour. The oil tank attached to the engine had a capacity of 9.6 litres, so the aircraft could not exceed six hours of flight in a row. For mechanics and pilots alike, the 8K50 was a rustic and reliable engine. As it did not need electrical generation to run, it was sometimes described as an 'oil boiler', as it only needed fuel to obtain thrust.

Access to the Atar was easy with the removal of the rear part of the fuselage. With no afterburner, the 8K50 was a short engine. (Frédéric Lert)

The Super Étendard's muscle: the Atar 8K50 jet engine. It was a sturdy engine with no reheat. (Frédéric Lert)

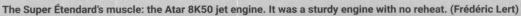

Chapter 2

The Super Étendard in Service

The official entry of the SUE into service with the French Navy was considered to be 28 June 1978. Indeed, it was on that date that the third production aircraft was officially handed over to the Aéronavale by the Dassault factory in Mérignac. However, aircraft No 3 actually went to the CEPA, together with aircraft No 4. At the same time, SUE production aircraft Nos 1 and 2 remained at the disposal of the CEV.

In fact, the first aircraft entering service into a flottille was the fifth production aircraft, which landed at Landivisiau Naval Air Station in September 1978. It joined the ranks of Flottille 11F, which had been operating the Étendard IVM for 15 years. A little less than four years had passed between the prototype's first flight in October 1974 and the aircraft entering service. Flottille 11F, callsign 'Kimono' ('K' being the 11th letter of the alphabet), was therefore the first to be re-equipped at the rate of one aircraft per month. It took one year to receive its full complement of 12 aircraft. The aircraft were widely available and the flottille trained its pilots quickly.

Pictured here, a Super Étendard cleared the deck of *Foch*. The splash behind the aircraft came from the bridle falling into the water. (ARDHAN)

From the Corsair to the SUE

Lieutenant-Commander Maurice Argouse, who was then the unit's commanding officer, remembered the transition:

> We started by training experienced Étendard IVM pilots, but they were quickly followed by younger pilots. We had a few minor weapon systems failures, but nothing extraordinary for such an advanced aircraft. We were a little annoyed in the first few weeks and then things quickly got back to normal. The former Étendard pilots, for whom navigation was quite an art, were outraged by the capabilities offered by the Super Étendard. They demanded that young people do every third flight without the inertial navigation system, honing their skills using more traditional navigation methods. But that was nonsense, because without the INS, you couldn't fly the Super Étendard. Very quickly we focused training on firing weapons, with the high level of precision that the use of the INS allowed.

Ramon Josa, an emblematic character of French Naval Aviation, remembered well what the commissioning of the Super Étendard could represent:

> I went from propeller-driven F-4U Corsair to the Étendard, then from the Étendard to the Super Étendard, after a short posting on Crusader. I believe the step was higher between the Étendard and the Super Étendard than between the F-4U Corsair and the Étendard [...] The way of flying and conducting the mission was totally upset, the Super Étendard belonged to a different century. With the Étendard, we finally had the same offensive weapons as on Corsairs: cannons, dumb bombs and a sight. We had certainly doubled the speed and added a small bombing calculator, but basically, the mission and the way it was conducted did not vary much [...] With the Super Étendard, we could now fly, navigate and attack in all weathers, day and night. It was a major development to which we had to adapt, and it was not always easy.

From 4–8 December 1978, a first embarkation on *Foch*, off the coast of Toulon, qualified a dozen pilots for daytime landing. For the first time, landing could be done using the HUD instead of the classic mirror landing system that was previously used exclusively. A giant, triangular sight was painted on the flight deck of the aircraft carriers to mark the point of aim precisely. The pilot's job was to maintain his slope cue based on the triangular sight, in order to maintain the correct landing slope.

The first production aircraft in a 'clean' configuration pictured right after its delivery to the French Navy. (ARDHAN)

Handover

In the spring of 1979, it was *Clemenceau*'s turn to receive the new aircraft for the first time. *Foch*'s sister-ship was modified the previous year with refitted workshops, ammunition bunkers transformed to receive tactical nuclear weapons, and the installation of Telemir equipment for INS synchronisation. Communications installations were also modernised, and some improvements were made to the living quarters. *Foch* underwent a similar upgrade process between July 1980 and August 1981. When it was commissioned, the SUE was still only equipped with its cannons, dumb bombs and rockets. It took a few more years for it to receive the AM39 Exocet anti-ship missile and the AN52 tactical nuclear bomb – two exceptional weapons that would fully distinguish the SUE from the Étendard.

The 'buddy-buddy' refuelling was a necessity to increase the range of the Super Étendard. (ARDHAN)

Super Étendard No 12, with a Douglas air-to-air refuelling pod. (ARDHAN)

 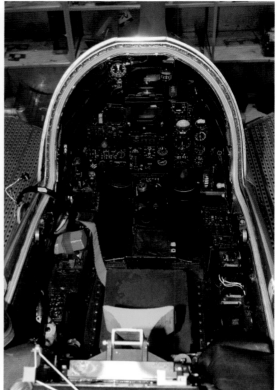

Above left and above right: The cockpit of the Super Étendard Modernisé Standard 5. The video display was right below the head-up display (HUD). (Frédéric Lert)

While developing the operational capabilities of the SUE, 11F trained the pilots of Flottille 14F, which would trade its F-8FN Crusaders for the new French aircraft. The 'One-Eyed Privateer' flottille (a reference to its emblem) received its first SUE in June 1979 and relinquished the air defence mission.

Created 25 years earlier during the Indochina War, 14F, callsign 'Negus', was brought back to its roots when training for maritime and land assaults. It was then flying Corsairs. The transition from Corsairs to SUEs was completed at the end of 1979. It then participated in the training of Argentinian pilots, the 17F – the third and final flottille equipped with the SUE – and, finally, the pilots of the 59S escadrille, a training unit that abandoned its last Étendard IVM in the summer of 1991. The 59S' training was the last mission of 14F, which was dissolved on 10 July 1991.

For its own part, the 17F received its first aircraft in September 1980. While it was still only half-equipped, the 'Quinquina' (as usual, the callsign starts with the 17th letter of the alphabet) took part in its first deployment in the Mediterranean at the beginning of 1981. The flottille was fully operational with the new aircraft in March of that year. As mentioned above, the 59S training squadron, based in Hyères, replaced the last of its Étendard IVMs in the summer of 1991, when it received eight SUEs. Six of these aircraft, which operated alongside a dozen CM175 Zéphyrs, came from 14F when it was disbanded. The other two aircraft came from 17F and 11F. Finally, it should be noted that the Flottille 16F was never equipped with the SUE; it continued its activity with the Étendard IVP until it disbanded on 28 July 2000.

In the early 1990s, the French Navy had around 45 SUEs in three frontline units, plus one training escadrille.

Right: **No fewer than 12 aircraft flew a Lorraine Cross formation (emblem of the Free French during World War Two) for an official ceremony in 1981. (ARDHAN)**

Below: **The first two SUEs (Nos 3 and 4) to reach Landivisiau were escorted by two F-8N Crusaders and a lone Étendard IV. (ARDHAN)**

Above: A flypast over USS *Kennedy* (CVN79) in the Mediterranean in 1980, with ten SUEs leading the pack in front of four Crusaders. (ARDHAN)

Left: No fewer than 21 SUEs (and two MS Parises and two Falcon 10s) were visible in this great shot taken in the early 1980s above Landivisiau Naval Air Base. (ARDHAN)

From the SUE to the SEM

The Super Étendard had always received a lot of attention from the French Navy, and several modernisation programmes enabled it to maintain its rank throughout its operational life, including in the demanding framework of coalition operations, in which the aircraft have occasionally been used. The experience feedback from the first engagements in Lebanon and the Persian Gulf led to a first series of measures aimed at improving the aircraft's self-protection. The SUE was equipped with the Barracuda jammer, the Phimat (a contraction of Philips and Matra) chaff launcher and an infrared flares launcher. The more complex modernisation programmes were, however, grouped into more ambitious projects, carried out during periods of major aircraft maintenance.

The plan to upgrade the SUE, which ultimately led to the development of the Super Étendard Modernisé (SEM), was launched at the beginning of the 1980s, shortly after the aircraft was put into service. In preference to a single upgrade project, the idea of continuous development in several stages (giving rise to different 'standards') was adopted. This way of doing things allowed for gradual modernisation, according to budgets, operational needs, feedback and technical opportunities. The modernisation programme to create the SEM was formally launched in 1986, and SUE Nos 8 and 68 were assigned to this programme, aiming for a SEM Standard 1.

Captured here was rush hour on *Foch*, with two SUEs waiting to be catapulted for a dusk mission. (Frédéric Lert)

A Super Étendard was marshalled to the catapult, with another SUE and a Crusader in tow. (Frédéric Lert)

SUE No 68 was one of five aircraft loaned to Iraq from 1983 to 1985. Returning from the Gulf, it did not rejoin a flottille. Modification work on the first aircraft began at Istres in 1988 and ended two years later. The aircraft took off for the first time on 5 October 1990, with Yves Kerhervé at the controls. The CEPA then created a SEM detachment in Istres at the beginning of 1991 to evaluate the aircraft and prepare for its entry into service. However, the evaluation of the first SEM (No 8) concluded that there was a need for additional work to finalise the development of the first standard. It was then decided to abandon Standard 1, take a step back and plan for a more potent Standard 2.

The industrialisation process was given to the Atelier Industriel de l'Aéronautique (AIA – aeronautical industrial workshop) of Cuers Pierrefeu and began in 1992. A total of 52 aircraft were upgraded (plus No 68, which remained a hybrid aircraft – part SUE, part SEM). The first production aircraft was delivered to the Navy on 8 June 1993, and 17F, the first re-equipped flottille, was officially declared operational with the 'new' aircraft in November 1995.

A new radar for a new life

The Standard 2 aircraft mainly benefitted from upgraded avionics, new cockpit ergonomics and a complete overhaul of the electric system. The instrument panel was reorganised, with a first application of the HTS (Hands on Throttle and Stick) concept, where the pilot could control the radar and the weapon system without releasing the throttle and the stick, which was useful in combat. The Thomson CSF120 collimator, with its rather limited functions, was replaced with a wide field HUD.

Left: The nose gear's shock absorber was overinflated to give the aircraft the correct angle on take-off. (Frédéric Lert)

Below: About to catch number one wire for a good landing. The white 'F' in the background was for *Foch*. (Frédéric Lert)

Facing the pilot, a new multi-function display (MFD) capable of displaying the imagery of external sensors replaced the old radar cathode-ray tube (CRT). This screen was identical to the one used on the Mirage 2000-5, but, strangely enough, it did not match the colour display. Navy pilots had to be satisfied with a monochrome display that only used different shades of green. The aircraft's navigation and attack system benefitted from the replacement of the UAT 40 main computer with the UAT 90; the latter was about six times more powerful and capable of 'interacting' with the equipment provided for the following standards.

Standard 2 also brought a major improvement through the replacement of the Agave radar by the Anemone from Thomson CSF (now Thales), optimised for the use of the AM39 Exocet and the ASMP nuclear missiles. The new radar was, therefore, a remarkable combination for meeting air-to-air, air-to-ground and air-to-surface needs. Its range was much greater than that of the Agave, with better resistance to jamming thanks to its frequency hopping capability. It also provided air-to-air capacity, including a Track While Scan mode, a mapping mode, and an efficient air-to-sea mode. The air-to-air mode was rated excellent by pilots who experienced Agave and a little above average by younger pilots lacking that benchmark. As an indication, it easily locked on targets 20nm (37km) away, while the Agave hardly exceeded 8nm (14km) on good days.

On the other hand, the Anemone gave the distance and altitude of a 'contact', without providing information on its speed and course. It also did not offer a 'look down' capability. In any case, the SEM could not carry and use any radar-guided air-to-air missiles. The aircraft's radar could tell if a target was within firing range for an infrared-guided Magic missile, but it was up to the pilot to ensure that the target telemetered by the radar and the one captured by the missile heat-seeker were one and the same.

Laser weapons for the SEM

All the aircraft upgraded to Standard 2 were not immediately equipped with the Anemone radar, and some had to fly for some time with the previous generation Agave. When the aircraft was withdrawn from service, it was still possible to find some Agaves on the shelves of the maintenance service; these radar were used as ballast when an Anemone had to be removed from an aircraft for maintenance. A Radar Adapter and Interface Box had to be used to install either an Agave or an Anemone in the nose of a SEM.

The Standard 3, which entered service in April 1997, provided the SEM with the capability to fire laser-guided weapons, AS30LS missiles (LS for 'Secured Laser') and bombs. With the 1,000kg Matra BGL 1000, then used by the Mirage 2000D of the Armée de l'air, being too heavy for the SEM, the sailors turned to Raytheon and ordered the GBU-12 fitted with the Paveway II guidance kits. Subsequently, the requirement to adapt the bomb to the aircraft carrier storage and handling

Taxiing towards the catapult with the right wing still folded. The heavy smoke coming from the boilers made a dramatic background. (Frédéric Lert)

Above: The SUEs had their wings folded on the carrier. Folding and unfolding was done manually by the deck crew. (Frédéric Lert)

Left: Seen here was the last instant before touch down on *Foch*, while the ship continued to steam full speed ahead. (Marine nationale)

requirements gave birth to the BLU-111 bomb, which was used in Afghanistan. The 125kg and 250kg CBEMS bombs completed the armament range. For the GBU-12s and BLU-111s, the standard configuration was initially one ammunition under each wing. The bomb adaptation to carry two bombs under one wing and an additional tank under the other only appeared with Standard 5.

Target laser designation was done with the Thomson-CSF ATLIS II pod. With a mass of 160kg, the pod was fitted under the fuselage and required the removal of the gun chassis for its transport. It allowed telemetry, target designation and automatic tracking. The image was projected on a screen in the cockpit, but it could also be recorded on a videotape.

Standard 3, however, showed a certain limitation, as the aircraft could not both fire the bomb and 'lase' it. In a patrol, the work was divided between an illuminator aircraft and a bomber aircraft. It was only with Standard 4 that the SEM, equipped with a new fire control system, could simultaneously perform both operations.

A standard for the 21st century

The objective of Standard 4 was first and foremost to give the SEM better self-protection. The aircraft received a SHERLOC P radar alert detector, replacing the old 'BF', which no longer fit the threats of the moment. Alkan flare launchers were mounted under the so-called 'point zero' under the wing, close to the fuselage. Each pylon could carry 90 40mm cartridges or 40 60mm cartridges. These pylons made the use of flares in the tail launcher, installed in the parachute housing, obsolete. The Barracuda detection and jamming pod and the Phimat chaff launcher completed the ECM suite. A centralised system coordinated the aircraft's self-protection, while providing the pilot with a complete overview of the tactical situation. Colour codes and specific symbology made it possible to, at a glance, appraise the nature of the threat, its intensity and its position relative to the aircraft. The other major innovation of Standard 4 is the use of the Chassis de Reconnaissance Marine (CRM) 280, which was housed in the fuselage, in place of the guns and ammunition. Eight CRMs were bought by the Navy and delivered to the flottilles from September 2000. The 'recce' capacity added to the SEM came in conjunction with the withdrawal from service of the last Étendard IVP from the 16F. Standard 4 SEMs also gained a GPS receiver, enabling precise updating of the INS.

A total of 47 SEMs were upgraded to Standard 4 in 2005 (four aircraft went directly from Standard 3 to Standard 5), but Standard 5, the ultimate level of modernisation of the aircraft, was already on the horizon. However, the SEM included an intermediate step, sometimes called Standard 4+, initially allowing the use of the Damocles laser pod to replace the ATLIS II. The Standard 5, of which there

SUEs and a Crusader shared the forward deck of *Foch* in the early 1990s. (Frédéric Lert)

were 33 modified aircraft plus No 14, which served as a development aircraft, benefitted from a cockpit upgrade, allowing the use of night vision goggles (NVGs). The aircraft gained a nighttime precision bombing capability, thereby filling an operational gap highlighted during operations in Kosovo in 1999, and even during the first engagements in Afghanistan three years later. The Aéronavale was the first to use the Damocles pod in France, with 15 units ordered. In addition to the nighttime firing capability, the Damocles also enabled firing at greater altitude, thanks to the increased power of its laser. The Damocles also carried a navigation Flir, an infrared pointer, a laser spot detector and an air-to-air reconnaissance mode, all of which provided the aircraft and its pilot with greater operational flexibility and situational awareness. The images provided are presented to the pilot on the HUD or the central MFD.

Above: Fitted with four unguided rocket pods, this Super Étendard displays heavy firepower against lightly defended targets. (Frédéric Lert)

Left: The Super Étendard was a small aircraft with a tight cockpit. (Frédéric Lert)

SEM No 13, seen here in 2005, was about to be catapulted from *Charles de Gaulle* with a Damocles laser pod. (Frédéric Lert)

Sometimes deck operations required some brutal strength. Here, the arresting cable had to be disengaged from the hook by pushing back SEM No 52. (Frédéric Lert)

After the landing, a SEM rolled to the end of the deck and cleared the landing spot. (Frédéric Lert)

SEM No 52 cleared the deck and the catapult bridle fell into the water. (Frédéric Lert)

Here, the pilot obeyed the hand signals and precisely positioned his SEM on the catapult. (Frédéric Lert)

The last second before touch down. This SEM flew with external wing tanks most of the time. (Frédéric Lert)

Last upgrades

Standard 5 (S5) also allowed the use of GBU-49 GPS-guided bombs. The theory was that the aircraft could carry two bombs under each wing. In practice, both to conserve autonomy and power, the load was limited to two bombs under one wing and a 1,100-litre tank under the other. The SEM S5 also inherited a new autopilot, which was able to maintain a heading and an attitude in climb, in descent and in turns (which the old automatic pilot could not do). It could also perform an altitude 'capture' in climb or descent and trim the aircraft automatically, but the management of navigation remained the responsibility of the pilot.

From 2002 onward, operations in Afghanistan resulted in the addition of several pieces of equipment on the SEM S5s, such as a Saturn encrypted radio supplementing the Have Quick, and the Fightacs digital pad.

All of these upgrades offered the SEM S5 a much appreciated versatility. However, the aircraft, which was completely replaced by the Rafale by 2015, was never offered a hypothetical 'Standard 6'. The pilots always regretted some shortcomings: absence of radar rallying for the Magic, absence of the L16 data link, non-integration of the MICA missile, and of course, the absence of any re-engine programme!

Left: Contrary to *Foch* and *Clemenceau,* which were fitted with four arresting cables, *Charles de Gaulle* only had three, which required a more precise landing. (Frédéric Lert)

Below: A Rafale M and a Super Étendard Modernisé pictured side by side on *Charles de Gaulle* in November 2005. (Frédéric Lert)

The weight of the aircraft was indicated to the pilot before being catapulted. (Frédéric Lert)

Right: Until 2016, the SEMs shared the deck of *Charles de Gaulle* with the Rafale Ms (visible in the background). (Frédéric Lert)

Below: This SEM was about to land, with two dispensers used to carry BAVAR F4 training bombs under its wing. (Frédéric Lert)

Rafales and SEMs shared the deck as *Charles de Gaulle* turned to face itself towards the wind. (Frédéric Lert)

Aircraft No 49 pictured moving from its spot toward the catapult. Note the additional air intake open on the fuselage. (Frédéric Lert)

Above left: As the Super Étendard was not a powerful aircraft, it had to be light and thin. (Frédéric Lert)

Above right: On *Charles de Gaulle*, Rafales and SEMs used two different methods with the catapult. However, it took only a few seconds to change the 'shuttle' and switch from one system to the other. (Frédéric Lert)

Right: This SEM was pushed back by hand over a short distance in order to put the front wheel back in line. (Frédéric Lert)

Above: SEM No 49 left its spot, while the Rafale M in the background waited for its turn to start taxiing. (Frédéric Lert)

Left: The process of teaming SEMs and Rafale Ms was designed to be an interim solution, running only until the retirement of the first. The Rafales are now the only fighter aircraft operating from *Charles de Gaulle* (in the background). (Marine nationale)

All the flottille pilots were lined up for the last catapulting of one of their colleagues. The 'shooter' used a sword, instead of the traditional green flag. (Marine nationale)

Above: No fewer than 13 SEMs and Rafale Ms were used for this flypast with all the hooks down. (Frédéric Lert)

Right: A room with a view! This SEM reached the end of the deck during a catapult launch, as seen by the pilot. (DR)

Below: Pictured flying inverted in a four-ship formation – this was not an everyday stunt for the SEM. (DR)

SEMs Nos 1 and 51 received special markings for the type's retirement. Interestingly enough, No 1 was painted in the same colors it had when entering service, 38 years before. (Alexandre Paringaux)

Below: Pictured on 12 July 2016, SEM No 1 taxied back after its last air display. It was the same day as all SEM retirement at Landivisiau Naval Air Base. (Frédéric Lert)

Above: No 51, seen here, in sober retirement colours at Landivisiau, on 12 July 2016. (Frédéric Lert)

Right: Three aircraft took part in the retirement ceremony on 12 July 2016. While two were specially painted, SEM No 41 showed its regular camouflage. (Frédéric Lert)

Below: The beautifully painted SEM No 1, still flying after nearly 40 years of service. The refuelling probe was out and the hook was down. (Frédéric Lert)

The nightlife of the Super Étendard

When the Super Étendard entered service, the French Navy had very limited experience in night operations from aircraft carriers. The SNCASE Aquilon (French licence-built version of de Havilland Sea Venom) led the way on *Clemenceau*, but very carefully. The Étendard itself had played the extreme sport of night deck operation sparingly. Two pilot qualification campaigns were undertaken in 1969 and 1970, before the night capacity was finally set aside, as the risks were deemed excessive on the aircraft without radar, compared to the benefits that could be derived from it. In the end, the Crusaders were the most active in this area, although, here too, caution dominated; it took several months, or even years in some cases, for a pilot to go from a daytime to a nighttime qualification.

The first night landing of a Super Étendard was carried out on 14 January 1980, by Lieutenant-Commander Robert Feuilloy. The pilot was considered a specialist in the field, having benefited from an exchange programme with the VA-46 in the US Navy. He had logged 264 deck landings with the A-7B Corsair II, including 103 at night. This was in addition to the 16 night landings he previously accumulated on the French Crusader; undeniably, Robert Feuilloy was the most experienced French pilot in this discipline. On the evening of 14 January, he headed for *Foch*, landed safely and entered history.

A safe aircraft to land at night

In the opinion of the pilots, the ergonomics of the SUE made night flight relatively comfortable. The organisation of the cockpit, its lighting, and, of course, the presence of a radar and a high-performance navigation suite opened wide the doors to night operations.

The use of NVGs came with the Standard 4 aircraft. NVGs were helpful when flying low and fast, or for spotting laser pointers. (Collection Baron)

The SUE allowed the pilot to choose between two methods for deck landing: either with the HUD or, more conventionally, the landing mirror. Both methods were, in fact, tolerated, with the pilot announcing over the radio which one he wanted to use. However, the mirror was favoured for daytime operations. With the HUD, the pilot simply used a sight painted on the oblique deck of the carrier. This target appeared as a simple white line when the pilot was flying a 3.5-degree glide. At night, the use of the sight, which was made phosphorescent by ultra-violet lighting, allowed the pilot to align himself on the glide at a great distance from the deck, well beyond that enabled by the mirror. As long as the auto-throttle functioned correctly, the pilot was then in a very good configuration.

This sight was later refined and given the shape of a triangle, enabling the pilot to better counter the traditional sinking of the aircraft seconds before hitting the deck. After their overhaul at the end of the 1980s, *Clemenceau* and *Foch* were subsequently fitted with lights embedded in the flight deck. SEM night operations quickly became routine, with the night landings qualification accessible to operational pilots with around 600 hours of flight time on the SEM.

NVG operations
The first piloting and firing tests with NVGs on the SEM date back to the end of 1987, when Commander Wilmot Roussel, 11F's Commanding Officer, took advantage of a detachment in Djibouti to simulate rocket firing against a derelict lighthouse. 'I was just as comfortable as if it was in broad daylight', he remembered. His wingman, who stayed at altitude but saw him plunge towards the sea in the dark, was much more worried.

However, the use of NVGs was only standard with the SEM S4 or S5 when the cockpits were duly modified for 'low level of light' use. It was then possible to hold the formation flight (position lights off) and navigate at very low altitude and very high speed, skimming the sea level at night.

In close air support missions, the main use for NVGs was to enable the location of laser pointers, operating in infrared wavelengths, used by ground troops to designate targets. On the other hand, the poor appreciation of distances induced by the NVGs formally prohibited their use on landing with the French Navy. They were then wisely stored in their case, just like during the catapulting.

Performing a touch-and-go on an American carrier. The wires had been removed to avoid any possibility of the aircraft catching one by accident, as it would have been impossible to catapult the SEM back off the American carrier. (US Navy)

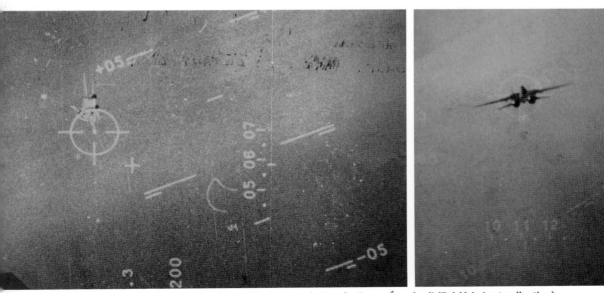

Above left and above right: An F-14 pictured in the crosshairs of a Super Étendard! (Frédéric Lert collection)

A former French Navy F-4U Corsair led the pack, with four Super Étendards in tow. (ARDHAN)

Theoretically, a Super Étendard could refuel an F-14 Tomcat. However, a thirsty Tomcat would need more fuel than the SUE could deliver. (ARDHAN)

A low flypast from a Super Étendard above the deck of USS *Nimitz* (CN68). The relationship between the US and the French navies has always been cordial. (ARDHAN)

A KA-6D Intruder refuelling two Super Étendards. (ARDHAN)

Above and left: For the September 2007 Nato Tiger Meet (later renamed the Arctic Tiger Meet) held in Norway, Flottille 11F sent two SEMs, beautifully painted with a Siberian tiger design. (Benjamin Vinot Prefontaine)

In 2008, 11F went for a dramatic black and red paint scheme for the Tiger Meet, which took place that year in Landivisiau. SEM No 71, shown in the background, was the last one ever built. (Benjamin Vinot Prefontaine)

In 2010, SEM No 23 was specially painted to celebrate 100 years of French Naval Aviation. (Marine nationale)

Chapter 3

The Aircraft and Its Missions

The Étendard was designed as a natural extension of the aircraft carrier. The SUE followed the same logic, and it was, therefore, a relatively small and compact aircraft. It was also light, so that it could be launched from the *Clemenceau* and the *Foch*, whose catapults were only 50m long (75m on *Charles de Gaulle*, which succeeded them). Its maximum mass was 12.4 tonnes on the catapult, with relatively little internal fuel: 2.5 tonnes (or 3,270 litres) divided between wing structural fuel tanks and fuselage bladder tanks. The SUE could also use two drop tanks of 600 litres or 1,100 litres under the wings (the 1,100 litres was qualified several years after the aircraft was put into service) and another 600-litre tank under the fuselage, which made a maximum of 6,070 litres possible. To leave some room for the weapons, however, a wing tank had to be removed, which dropped the maximum fuel load to less than 5,000 litres. On the other hand, the Super Étendard gained some advantages from its small size compared to its contemporaries, the aircraft was manoeuvrable and relatively difficult to see from a distance. The low thrust of its engine also made it a 'cold' aircraft, with a weak infrared signature, and difficult to spot for infrared-guided missiles.

Significant progress

Any young pilot getting to know the SUE began by taking good note of the differential braking system. When taxiing, the trajectory was managed by alternating the brakes to the right and left, and any lack of experience was easily recognised by the zigzag of the aircraft on the runways. Once in flight, the aircraft was defined as stable and responsive, and very pleasant to fly. With the SUE, Dassault once again consolidated its excellent reputation in terms of flight controls. The Étendard was clearly underpowered, which could be dangerous at a high angle of attack or low speed, constantly operating very close to its stall speed when landing on a carrier. Unlike other aircraft, which shake before

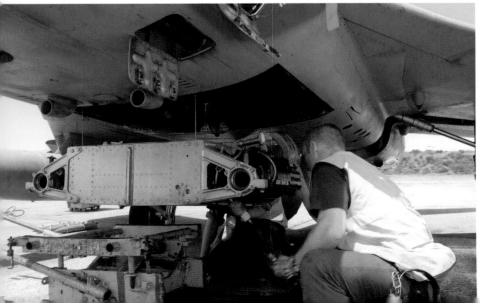

Armourers removed the gun chassis during a firing campaign in 2010. Removing the chassis enabled the aircraft to be fitted with the control box for the Exocet or a nuclear mission. (Frédéric Lert)

SEM No 10 launched with a Douglas refuelling pod. (Frédéric Lert)

Seen here at rush hour on *Charles de Gaulle*, Rafales and SEMs took turns on the catapults. (Marine nationale)

stalling, the Étendard 'shook after crashing down', its pilots quipped. From this point of view, the Super Étendard marked significant progress. Not that the aircraft was Formula 1 – with 5,000kg of thrust, the Atar 8K50 offered a thrust-to-weight ratio of no more than 0.5, not enough to chase a MiG-21 in a vertical climb, but enough to fire bombs with laser guidance or sow panic in an enemy naval formation with a volley of Exocet missiles. The aircraft was also cut out for low flying and its pilots considered it as manoeuvrable as the Mirage 2000D or N two-seaters, fitted with their huge 2,000-litre external tanks. Beyond flight level (FL) 200, however, the Super Étendard ran out of steam, although its generously sized wing allowed worry-free refuelling at FL290.

The SUE was a no-brainer on the catapult. Overinflating its nose gear shock-absorber gave it the right angle of attack and, with a well-adjusted trim, the aircraft flew on its own when exiting the deck. The pilot just needed to gently catch the stick when leaving the deck to keep the aircraft in a good attitude. When landing at night or in bad weather, guided by the on-board controller, the pilot displayed the desired angle of attack, and the auto-throttle automatically regulated the engine to maintain it. The pilot could, however, choose to regain control of the auto-throttle at any time. The first SUEs only had the very simple autopilot inherited from the Étendard, which only allowed altitude and heading held with two-axis control: pitch and roll. The autopilot was itself controlled by an analogue computer, fed by the information given by a simple longitudinal accelerometer. The altitude hold function was used, for example, in maritime assaults characterised by long overflights at very low height above the waves. A more sophisticated autopilot appeared with the Standard 5.

Left: Photographed in the early 1980s, a Super Étendard was loaded with 68mm rockets. Operating unguided rockets from *Charles de Gaulle* was forbidden, as the French Navy felt it unsafe to have those ammunitions on a nuclear vessel. (ARDHAN)

Below: A 400kg free-fall bomb hoisted onto a Super Étendard aboard *Clemenceau*, circa 1981. (ARDHAN)

In the cockpit

The SUE's cockpit was relatively narrow and taller pilots were a little stuck at shoulder level. When it entered service, the Super Étendard offered its pilot a Martin Baker 4A seat, derived from the Mk4 of the Étendard. The Mk4 was a rather rustic seat, requiring the pre-ejection of the canopy before it could leave the aircraft. This resulted in a one-second delay between triggering the handle and the actual ejection. The Mk4 required (at zero height) a minimum speed of 90kt to be effective. The Martin Baker 4A fitted on the SUE allowed the pilot to eject directly through the canopy, which resulted in a faster ejection sequence, but it kept the same limitations in terms of height and ejection speed. The modernisation of the SUE into the SEM, enabled the aircraft to receive the SEMMB Mk6 seat, offering the 'zero zero' capacity, an ejection possible at zero speed and height. This seat was originally fitted to the Argentinian SUEs.

When it entered service, the SUE boasted a very basic armament. It was very similar to that of the Étendard for air-to-ground missions — two 30mm DEFA guns supplied with 120 rounds each (at a rate of 1,250 rounds per minute, each gun had barely 6 seconds of firing), free-fall bombs of 250kg and 400kg, high-drag bombs and rockets. At the other end of the spectrum, the flottilles were gradually equipped with the AM39 Exocet anti-ship missile and then with the AN52 tactical atomic bomb from January 1981. In the air-to-air domain, the SUE could also use its two on-board cannons, and it received the Matra Magic 1 infrared guided missile (later replaced with the much better Magic 2), which replaced the Sidewinder that fitted the Étendard. The 68mm SNEB rockets, carried in pod of 18 projectiles, were withdrawn from service when the SEM migrated to *Charles de Gaulle* because they were incompatible with the safety requirements on board the nuclear aircraft carrier. In the last years of active duty, the high-drag and the 400kg free-fall bombs were also no longer considered for real life operations. The 250kg free-fall bombs were also no longer used in operation, but pilots continued to practice with them, and the capability was therefore still present in theory.

An interesting view of a Super Étendard, pictured here as it rolled toward the catapult and was armed with a Magic infrared missile. (ARDHAN)

Left: 68mm rocket pods were fitted on this Super Étendard, which was photographed operating from Landivisiau Naval Air Base. (Frédéric Lert)

Below: The Flottille 14F, which flew the Super Étendard from 1979 onwards, acted as an Operational Conversion Unit until it was disbanded in 1991. (Frédéric Lert)

Bottom: Thanks to the Exocet missile, the Super Étendard became a fearsome attack aircraft in anti-shipping missions. (Frédéric Lert)

Complexification

The firing sequence aboard an early 1980s SUE was relatively straightforward and took place in a still uncluttered cockpit. Placed under a radar screen, the armament selection station (PSA) enabled the choice of which armament was used first. The Armament Command Post (PCA), placed on the right-side console, enabled pilots to configure the firing sequence and, in particular, the intervals during the firing of bombs or rockets. The only thing the pilot needed to do was to place the 'master arm' on 'ON', aim and fire with the trigger on the stick.

Right: A GBU-12 Paveway III guided bomb was prepared during a firing exercice from Cazaux Air Force Base, southern France, in June 2010. (Frédéric Lert)

Below: Bavar F4 training bombs were loaded onto a SEM during a bombing campaign in June 2010. (Frédéric Lert)

The addition of above-standard equipment, linked to the use of an increasingly extensive range of weapons, gradually cluttered up the instrument panel and the side consoles. At the same time, the firing sequence became much more complex, with the first use of laser-guided weaponry.

The use of the laser designation pod was done via a control box placed on the left of the dashboard. A 'joystick' placed on the engine throttle, under the thumb, controlled the movement of the aim of the pod and the capture of the target (the joystick was also used for radar control). The target was illuminated via another command, this time placed directly under the middle finger, still on the throttle (this command also allowed targets to be designated in single bomb mode). The image obtained by the pod was displayed on the radar screen in a gradient of green. The laser coding armament box allowed the laser code of the bomb to be entered into the pod via three rotating knobs. The same code was entered by the armourers on the bomb simply by operating the coding wheels with a screwdriver. Of course, the codes entered in the laser coding armament box and on the bomb fired had to be identical so that the ammunition could 'see' the laser spot thus coded.

On the right-hand console, the armament command post was completed with a removable box fitted at the height of the seat and enabled the insertion of coordinates used for the GPS-guided GBU-49. The removable box was, in turn, completed by an Armament Guidance Box (BGA) or a Bomb Display Screen (EVB) at the top right of the dashboard. The BGA was used to set the terminal trajectory of the AM39 Exocet, while the EVB showed the range of GPS-guided bombs.

In June 2007, the integration of the hybrid guided GBU-49, GPS and/or laser on the Standard 5 aircraft added a little more workload for the pilot, who had to prepare the bomb on the EVB, follow the procedure linked to the release (involving the inertial unit, the PSA and PCA) and then illuminate the target in the case of mixed GPS and laser guidance.

In order to limit programme costs, the controls for using the GBU-49 bomb were not integrated with the rest of the weapon system. Two new Enhanced Paveway Avionics Kit (EPAK) boxes therefore appeared in the cockpit: the first on the right console to set the parameters and the second, a display, placed on the frame of the windshield, facing the pilot. Thanks to its two guidance modes, the GBU-49

Even when they were operating on firm ground, Navy technicians worked with the same equipment as when they were on an aircraft carrier. (Frédéric Lert)

offered greater operational flexibility, with the possibility of firing several bombs in bursts with a deflection, and by choosing the arrival routes of the bombs. The laser-guided bomb still had to be fired in the direction of the target like a conventional bomb. The laser guidance simply provided precision on impact.

Bomb loads and missiles

In addition to its two DEFA guns, the Super Étendard was equipped with five hardpoints, to which were added the two so-called 'zero' points used for the flare launchers. The result of the large number of qualified weapons on the aircraft was an equally impressive number of possible combinations.

The guns were placed in a chassis in the central part of the fuselage. The chassis was removed when necessary to gain mass, or, more simply, to gain space to house the electronic boxes of certain armaments, such as the ASMP nuclear missile or the AM39 Exocet. The gun chassis could also give way to the reconnaissance CRM 280 nacelle or to the laser designation pod. The central hardpoint under the fuselage could receive either an additional 600-litre tank, an in-flight Douglas refuelling nacelle (with a mass of 390kg), two conventional 250kg bombs or the laser designation pod (ATLIS II or Damocles). The inner points under the wing had a loading capacity of 1,100kg. They could receive additional tanks of 625 litres or 1,100 litres (450kg and 800kg, respectively) or offensive weaponry, or a mixture of the two. The configuration most often practiced in Afghanistan combined a 1,100-litre tank under one wing and one or two guided 250kg bombs under the other, with an autonomy of about 1.5hrs at medium altitude. In-flight refuelling allowed autonomy to be increased to 6 hours, the maximum authorized by the Atar reactor's oil reserve. In operation and in a tactical context, refuelling was required approximately every hour in order to keep sufficient reserves for return to base in the event of a problem during refuelling.

During the SEM's last operational years, 125kg and 250kg free-fall bombs were no longer used, and the preferred air-to-ground weapon was the guided bomb. Several models coexisted: the 125kg or 250kg MBDA CBEMS, both of which were equipped with Raytheon's Paveway II laser guidance kit. Also

Pictured landing back on *Charles de Gaulle* from a close air support mission, a SEM used a Damocles targeting pod. (Frédéric Lert)

The Super Étendard was also tested with powerful 100mm rockets. SUE No 35 carried a special modified fuel tank on the centerline, with high-speed cameras to film the firing. (VG)

equipped with this guidance kit, the GBU-12 was almost exclusively reserved for use from land-based operations. This ammunition, built around a 250kg Mk82 bomb body, was replaced on the aircraft carrier by the BLU-111 of identical mass. It had the advantage of being made less sensitive to attacks of all kinds that may be suffered on a carrier – fire on board, nearby detonations, mechanical shocks, aging, omnipresent electromagnetic fields. The BLU-111 was itself supplemented on the Standard 5 aircraft by the 250kg GBU-49, with the hybrid GPS/laser guidance system. Still under the inner hardpoints, the AM39 missiles and nuclear weapons (AN52, then ASMP and ASMP-A) were preferably carried under the right wing while the AS-30LS laser guided missile was carried indifferently under the left or right wing. The outer hardpoints had a maximum loading capacity of 450kg. They could each receive a rocket pod, a self-protection Magic missile or, more commonly, an electronic countermeasures pod. With the Standard 4 came the flare dispensers located under the wing, close to the fuselage, on the 'hardpoint zero'.

The Super Étendard and the Exocet: the perfect couple!
The Super Étendard earned its legendary status thanks to the deadly couple it formed with the AM39 Exocet anti-ship missile. This imposing missile, 4.69m long and 655kg, largely conditioned the development of the Super Étendard weapons system, which was organised around the Agave and then the Anemone radar. The Exocet missile was carried under the right wing, its mass being offset by the systematic carrying of an additional 1,100-litre tank under the left wing. The operational range of a Super Étendard was approximately 400km without in-flight refuelling, if the entire mission was conducted at low altitude. With a 'high-low-high' flight profile, with transit to the target occurring at a more economical altitude, the range could approach 600km. The maximum range of the AM39 was

around 60km, if fired at altitude and with good horizontal speed, to provide it with the maximum kinetic energy. A launch from altitude zero, just above the waves, would obviously result in a shorter range. Either way, the Exocet adopted a sea-skimming flight right above the waves, to delay detection and prevent interception.

The origin of the Exocet's programme dates back to 1969, and the first missile to emerge was the MM38, which was fired from ships. A former flottille commanding officer recalled:

At the end of the '60s, it was understood that attacking ships could no longer be carried out with bombs and rockets. Ships were increasingly able to defend themselves with radar-guided artillery and anti-aircraft missiles. So, we had to find a way to strike from a distance and with precision so that we did not all become suicide bombers. As fighter jets became very expensive, it was also important for our leaders that we brought them back in good condition after the mission. By allowing precise and remote firing, the anti-surface missile was the idea of the century!

Right: On *Clemenceau*, Super Étendard No 6 carried an AM39 Exocet for test purposes. In the background, the French Riviera coastline can be seen. (Aerospatiale)

Below: Landing with an Exocet was not an easy task, especially when the fuel tank under the left wing was empty. However, it was not an impossible one. (Aerospatiale)

To obtain an effective missile, however, it was necessary to work on the rocket engine (offering ranges of several dozens of kilometres), the miniaturised inertial units that guaranteed good precision at long range, and a seeker, also miniaturised, that allowed the missile to lock onto its target at the end of the flight. Putting these essential bricks together, along with an appropriate military payload, made it possible to imagine and create a missile capable of autonomously striking ships at great distances, up to the sea horizon and even beyond. The idea was good, and a race ensued between the French missile manufacturers. Nord Aviation (which would later become Aerospatiale and then MBDA) won the day by successfully developing its MM38 in record time, between 1969 and 1972.

One of the Exocet's strengths was its autonomous guidance mode, the development of which benefited directly from the research efforts made for the development of the French Pluton tactical nuclear missile. In its MM38 version, the Exocet indeed used the same inertial components and the same calculation techniques.

The development of the Super Étendard, equipped with a radar and an inertial unit capable of initialising the missile before its autonomous flight, then catalysed the development of a version launched by aircraft: the AM39.

In order to carry the Exocet under the wing of the Super Étendard, while contending with constraints on size and mass during catapulting (and possibly when landing) and avoiding burning the wing of the aircraft at the time of firing, major evolutions of the MM38 were required. The size of the missile was reduced, its aerodynamic profile optimised and, in order not to impair its range, its structure was also lightened. The strengthening of its on-board equipment also allowed it to withstand the limitations of operations on aircraft carriers and, in particular, catapulting and landing shocks. Development of the missile was rapid, although the missile did not arrive in flottilles until several months after the SUE. In the meantime, the pilots had plenty of time to simulate its use with their radar.

The first test firing of the AM39 took place in 1976, and the missile was declared operational with the French Navy four years later. When it entered service, the missile introduced a definite breakthrough in maritime combat, as the countermeasures against this self-guided projectile, which flew in the high subsonic, low over the waves, were ill-defined. The formidable reputation of the Exocet should not, however, erase the developmental difficulties. The first three test firings trialled

Catapulting with a test AM39 in the late 1970s was SUE No 31. In the background, the always present Alouette III 'Pedro' was ready to assist should the pilot have to eject. (Aerospatiale)

The rear view of an AM39 Exocet missile and its rocket engine. Note that the missile is not yet connected to the launch pylon. (Frédéric Lert)

with frontline flottilles from 1983, undoubtedly carried out at maximum range, all ended in failure. The missiles were correctly dropped, and ignition went off correctly, but the flight ended prematurely, possibly owing to a problem with the propellant unit. It was a period of doubt for the French Navy, which had invested heavily in the SUE-Exocet couple. On the other hand, Argentines and Iraqis obtained resounding successes in operation a short while later.

At the end of their operational career, the French Navy's SEMs had the possibility of firing two versions of the AM39: the block 7 and the block 8. The latter version offered more possibility of manoeuvres in terminal phase and an increased resistance to deception. However, the firing procedure had remained unchanged since the missile was put into service; firing was generally carried out at a very low altitude, around 300ft, with the missile falling about ten meters before igniting its rocket engine.

Prior to firing, the pilot transmitted the coordinates of an 'entry door' to the missile, within which was the target acquisition window for the missile seeker. In other words, once it was launched, the missile automatically directed itself to a point in space. Once this point was reached, it turned on its own radar and searched for the most promising target, trying not to be deceived by the decoys. In the meantime, the launch aircraft had made a sharp turn to return to its base as soon as the missile was released.

The anti-shipping mission, which could represent 50 per cent of the training for Super Étendard pilots at the turn of the century, later gave way to close air support missions with precision bombs. Anti-shipping training remained, however, a high priority during embarkations on the aircraft carrier, both for the benefit of the pilots and the crews of the ships acting as the targets. The simulation of anti-surface attacks was facilitated by the fact that it could be done without a training missile, the whole firing sequence being simulated with only the black boxes carried in the aircraft.

Ship hunting with the AM39 Exocet

First Lieutenant Rémi F remembered the following:

The SEM's Anemone radar performed significantly better than the Agave [the SUE's radar] it replaced. In air-to-sea mode, you could see everything in the forward sector within a radius of up to 100 nautical miles. In air-to-air, we also gained [ability] compared to the SUE, but without achieving breathtaking performance!

In anti-ship missions, we worked in close collaboration with the maritime patrol, Breguet Atlantique. We flew very low above the sea, radar off to escape enemy detection. Over the radio, the Breguet gave us a description of the radar image they had, that was before the data link. It was a very codified dialogue that allowed us to reconstruct the 'surpic', alias 'surface picture': the tactical situation on the sea. We knew then that in such and such a sector and at such a distance there was such and such an objective. We scribbled a sketch on our note pad attached to the thigh. The missile had to be prepared before firing: it had to be preheated, and we had to be certain that it was receiving the position information provided by the aircraft.

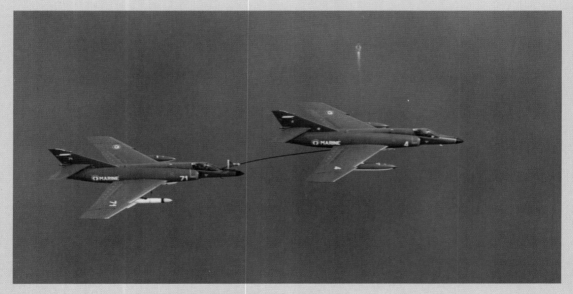

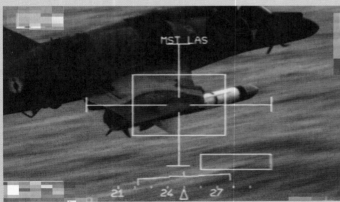

Above: 'Buddy-buddy' refuelling was the best way to extend the operational range of the Super Étendard and its Exocet. (ARDHAN)

Left: Photographed sea skimming with an Exocet tucked under the wing, a SEM was seen from a laser designating pod. (Marine nationale)

When the missile was ready, we could unmask ourselves and launch the attack: we quickly climbed a few hundred meters, up to 2,000 or 3,000ft from the surface, we turned on the radar and we chose the target. If the preliminary work had been done well with the patrol aircraft, the 'surpic' given to us by our radar looked like what we had on the pad and we could quickly select the target on the radar, and 'lock' it before cutting the radar. It was also possible to turn off the radar without locking the target, so the target would not hear the electronic signal characteristic of a locking radar. When off, the Anemone radar had the ability to extrapolate the tracks seen, taking into account the information gathered on the direction and the speed of the echoes. If we saw that some tracks changed course between two radar scans, we knew it could be our targets zigzagging to escape.

The SEM's Anemone radar also gave us a clear view of the situation with synthetic symbology showing the distance to the target and its size. This was a marked improvement over the Agave, which only showed us a vague display on the radar screen. A small echo on the screen could actually hide a large boat, and vice versa: the Agave was much more sensitive to electronic countermeasures than the Anemone, which was 'hardened'. And the SEM's radar warned us when it was experiencing interference, which was not the case with the SUE. Anti-shipping warfare is difficult but fascinating. With the SEM we were finally on a level playing field with the military ships we were attacking. Previously with the Super Étendard, it was a bit like suicide missions.

A very rare sight of two simultaneous Exocet launches, seen from a third aircraft. (Marine nationale)

Seen here was a low-level, simulated attack on a French frigate. Note how the 100mm gun of the ship is pointed towards the aircraft! (Marine nationale)

The Super Étendard and the atomic bomb

As had already happened with the US Navy, the idea of carrying an atomic bomb on an aircraft carrier gained ground within the French Navy in the 1960s, in an attempt to give it prominent stature. Tests were carried out with the Étendard and the AN22 bomb, but it was not until the entry into service of the Super Étendard and the AN52, with a maximum 25kt yield, that the atomic weapon became operational on a French aircraft carrier. The AN52, designed to answer the need of the French Air Force's Tactical Air Force (Fatac) Mirage IIIE and Jaguar, was 4m 20cm long and weighted 455kg. The first deliveries to the Armée de l'air were made in 1972. Three years later, the decision was made to equip the Aéronavale and the future Super Étendard with it.

The French Navy reportedly had a stockpile of 24 bombs placed at its disposal. However, these weapons were stored with those of the Armée de l'air, under the control of the latter. At the start of the 1980s, the ammunition stores of *Clemenceau* and *Foch* were adapted to receive four or five bombs.

Above: It was essential that the Super Étendard could land back on the carrier with the AN52 atomic bomb (the one seen here was a CEP52 training device). (ARDHAN)

Left: A close-up of the CEP52 training device. (ARDHAN)

Carried under the right wing, the AN52 was operational in 1980 and the Force d'Action Navale Nucléaire (FANu) was created.

To familiarise themselves with the use of the weapon, the first navy pilots trained with the Armée de l'air squadrons also using the AN52.

The training was also done with the CEP52 exercise container, which was the same shape and mass as the weapon. A housing in the container made it possible to carry and drop exercise bombs, reproducing the ballistics of the real weapon. As the AN52 was too large to fit centrally under the fuselage, it was mounted under the SUE's right wing, with a 1,100-litre fuel tank placed under the left wing. Catapulting was easy, with the aircraft correctly balanced with the bomb on the right and the full tank on the left. Landing back on a carrier was another story if, by extraordinary circumstances, a weapon had to be brought back on board, and the fuel tank under the left wing had been emptied or dropped.

'I did two deck landings with the AN52's mock-up and an empty fuel tank', remembered Admiral Blanvillain. 'Everybody on the ship was very interested to see if I was going to break the aircraft or not. In fact, the asymmetrical configuration was handled without too much problem.'

It is also notable that the French Navy did not drop any live weapons from the French Pacific nuclear test centre, while the Air Force launched two: the first one with a Mirage IIIE in 1973 and the second one with a Jaguar the following year.

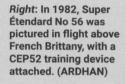

Right: In 1982, Super Étendard No 56 was pictured in flight above French Brittany, with a CEP52 training device attached. (ARDHAN)

Below: In 2008, a Super Étendard was shown to the French War School attendees, with an ASMP nuclear missile attached. (Frédéric Lert)

Launching the AN52 from the SUE followed the same rules as with the Armée de l'air aircraft: either in horizontal flight, or in a 35 degree climb with a ballistic trajectory. In both cases, the weapon was slowed down by a parachute as it descended, to allow time for the aircraft to clear away.

A quick glance at a map makes it possible to imagine what the targets of the carrier battle group cruising in the Mediterranean could have been: the former Yugoslavia, Bulgaria or Romania, for example. In short, the entire southern flank of the former Warsaw Pact, with the USSR itself largely out of reach. Flying a nuclear raid and opening a corridor into the enemy's defences would have undoubtedly required full engagement of the carrier air group. Another use of the bomb, predominantly maritime this time, could be imagined against the Soviet fleet in the Mediterranean, again mobilising most of the carrier air assets.

The exercises organised in the 1980s developed into complex assaults, mobilising around 20 Super Étendards, four Crusaders in support and a patrol of two Breguet Alizé for scouting. The SUE's armada carried four atomic bombs and 15 Exocets. Firing volleys of Exocets in front of the nuclear raid would have disrupted the anti-aircraft defences enough to give the other aircraft a chance to approach their targets. However, for the pilots of the time, there was little doubt that the nuclear mission with the AN52 would have been a one-way ticket to hell.

The AN52 was withdrawn from service by the Navy in 1991. It was replaced by the ASMP missile, which the flottilles had begun to familiarise themselves with two years earlier. As with the AN52, the use of the weapon simply required the placement of a specific control box in the aircraft. The entry into service really revolutionised the nuclear mission, for the aircraft as well as for the target. For the former, chances of survival were greatly improved! For the latter, there was a virtual impossibility

There was little doubt that an ASMP missile with a non-nuclear payload would make a terrific anti-ship missile! (Frédéric Lert)

of defending against a missile arriving at supersonic speed (close to Mach 2) and the even greater difficulty of intercepting the aircraft carrying the missile before firing. The ASMP range exceeded 300km (after a high-altitude launch), and a little less than 100km after a launch at wave height.

The ASMP was 5m 30cm long, 40cm in diameter and weighed 850kg. It was, therefore, 70cm longer and 190kg heavier than an AM39 Exocet, which was already quite bulky under the wing of a Super Étendard. As with the AN52, a 1,100-litre fuel tank acted as a counterweight under the left wing. However, unlike the AN52, it was deemed impossible to land back on a carrier with the missile or even a mock-up.

As one pilot recalled:

> The operational use of the ASMP was no longer like that of the AN52. We were shooting from a long distance; our chances of survival were on the rise again! The missile went up very high, it reached Mach 3 in top speed in altitude. We also had the possibility of firing it at low altitude, skimming the waves, with less range and speed, but it was still practically impossible to intercept.

After its release, the ASMP accelerated to supersonic speed within seconds, thanks to its booster using the ramjet's feed channel as a combustion chamber. At the end of this first phase, the nozzle was released, the air inlets uncapped, and the ramjet took over for cruise propulsion. In addition to the range conferred, the ramjet offered the advantage of being able to adjust the thrust according to the desired flight profile. The missile was completely autonomous in navigation, the precision of its trajectory depending on the quality of its inertial guidance. No radio, radar or GPS readjustment in flight was required.

Super Étendard No 26 was photographed during a experimental flight with an ASMP mock-up. (Aerospatiale)

SEM No 26 was photographed as it flew over *Clemenceau* during the ASMP development. (Aerospatiale)

The nuclear mission using the SEM was abandoned in 2010, and the Rafale F3 took over with the ASMP-A missile. The ASMP-A, a modernised version of the ASMP, was even longer and reached a mass of 1,100kg and was only carried on the Rafale. Until this point, all SEMs had been theoretically capable of carrying the ASMP. Like the AN52 or other specialized weapons (AM39 Exocet, GBUs, etc) the missile only required the installation in the cockpit of a removable control box.

The punchy AS30L

The AS30L laser-guided missile entered service with the French Air Force in 1985, first on the Jaguar and then, starting in 1993, on the Mirage 2000D. Two years later, the missile became operational on the Super Étendard Modernisé.

The AS30L was a powerful missile whose relatively light warhead (240kg for a total mass of 520kg) was offset by its very high impact speed (over 1,000km/h), resulting in a very high kinetic energy and a strong penetrating power. However, the missile had certain handicaps, primarily a use limited to good weather and the need to be guided until the impact. Its range, about 10km, prevented its use against strongly defended targets. It basically behaved like a huge and powerful laser-guided rocket, boasting good precision and destructive power, but with limited manoeuvrability.

Up to the Standard 4 SEM, its firing was quite restrictive for the aircraft, which had to 'lase' the target: the pilot had to simultaneously fly his aircraft and control the laser aiming.

Before firing, the aircraft had to be brought into a very precise position to provide the weapon with the right momentum toward its target. The pilot would approach the target low over the ground, 300ft max, then pop up rapidly to 1,500ft, find the target through the laser pod, lock on it, fire the missile from 10km away and 'lase' the target until impact.

The rapid sequence required firing against a relatively large target, such as a building or a bridge. For more precision, and in order to get more time to study the target, the pilot could also choose to go into a slight dive from an altitude of 10,000ft above the ground. Things became easier with the Standard 5, when the missile could be guided from a 'buddy lasing' aircraft.

In the anti-shipping mission, the AS30L could also be used against a target that did not require the use of an Exocet. The inconvenience of having to guide the missile to impact could then become an advantage, as the pilot could choose the area of impact very precisely. This was on the condition, of course, that the ship was poorly defended so that the aircraft could approach to within 8–10km of the target.

The AS30L missile was first introduced on the Armée de l'air Mirage 2000Ds in 1993. It reached the French Navy two years later. (Matra)

In 1999, during Operation *Allied Force*, two AS30L missiles were fired against ammunition depots on Ponikve Airport in Serbia. (Frédéric Lert collection)

Above: SEM No 45 is seen here in flight with two GBU-12s and a full ECM suite under its wings. (Frédéric Lert collection)

Left: The AS30L was often compared to a powerful guided rocket. Its main drawback was its short range, only 10km. (Frédéric Lert)

Seen taking off from Nîmes-Garons, a former naval air base, this trio of SEMs was about to blast some floating training targets in the Mediterranean with AS30s. (Baron)

This Super Étendard touched down with a speed slightly less than 130kt. Note the spoilers are barely visible on the right wing. (Frédéric Lert)

Right: The ATLIS laser designation pod for daylight operation. (Frédéric Lert)

Below: With four GBUs under its wing, but no external fuel tanks, the SEM could deliver heavy blows to some ground targets, albeit with a very limited 'playtime'. (Frédéric Lert)

The Super Étendard was an artist

The CRM 280 was a photographic pod that was placed in the fuselage in lieu of cannons and was equipped with two cameras: a Thales SDS250 electro-optical camera and an Omera 40 film camera (with traditional film). The SDS250 was optimized for low-level tactical reconnaissance and medium altitude; equipped with a 250mm focal length, it could shoot vertically or obliquely (with different settings) at a distance greater than 10km, the aiming done with an eyecup in the cockpit. Images obtained over a frequency, ranging from visible light to near infrared, were recorded on magnetic tape.

The Omera 40 was equipped with a traditional lens with a focal length of 75mm and was optimised for the low altitude. This allowed photography from horizon to horizon, with a 180-degree field of vision, at the maximum rate of ten frames per second. It could be equipped with colour or black and white films (approximately 400 frames), the latter being preferred for the best contrast and speed of development.

A wave-off for this Super Étendard, which carried a bulbous CRM 280 reconnaissance chassis behind the nose gear. (Marine nationale)

Chapter 4

The Wars of the Super Étendard

The Super Étendard was engaged in combat from the start of its career, starting off the coast of Lebanon and ending in Libya. The aircraft took part in thousands of missions with no losses.

The disintegration of the Lebanese state from 1975 led to the dispatch of a multinational interposition force under the UN banner. The French Navy took part in this deployment by maintaining several vessels off the Lebanese coast. All these successive operations took the code name *Olifant*. During the *Olifant XVII* mission in the autumn of 1983, 15 SUEs from 14F and 17F fleets were embarked on *Foch*. On 9 and 22 September, two artillery bombardments directed against the French embassy led to a retaliatory raid against the batteries, with eight SUEs armed with bombs and rockets and two photo-reconnaissance Étendard IVPs. One Étendard was hit by the anti-aircraft artillery but managed to land back on the aircraft carrier.

Foch then gave way to *Clemenceau* for the *Olifant XVIII* mission, which began on 6 October 1983 and brought together SUEs from all three flottilles. The mission was to protect the multinational security force in Beirut. On 23 October, a double bomb attack killed 241 American and 58 French soldiers. A retaliatory raid on a Hezbollah barracks, south of Baalbek, was mounted on 17 November.

Alongside the *Olifant* missions, the Mediterranean fleet patrolled the Libyan coast in September 1984. This was a deterrent mission, called *Mirmillon*, intended to weigh against Libya, whose interventionist aims in Chad were problematic for France. The SUEs embarked on the *Foch*, having been regularly trained to conduct night raids, which ultimately did not take place.

In 1987 and 1988, 11F and 17F were sent to the Arabian Sea as part of Operation *Prométhée*. The purpose was to ensure the safety of merchant ships targeted in the Iran-Iraq War. The aircraft carrier

The moment of truth pictured in November 1982: Super Étendard No 32 rolled to the catapult with six 400kg bombs to attack some Hezbollah barracks in Lebanon. (ARDHAN)

The SUEs used a special pylon to carry two 400kg bombs under the fuselage. The proximity of the target made the use of external fuel tanks unnecessary. (ARDHAN)

On 22 September 1983, a pilot climbed into his aircraft for the mission against a Syrian target in Lebanon. The small box on the right held the aircraft's safety pins. (ARDHAN)

sailed mainly in the Gulf of Aden and the Arabian Sea. Two years later came the First Gulf War. The carrier air group remained on alert but did not take part in the war.

Yugoslavia and Kosovo

Starting in mid-1991, the dismantling of Yugoslavia resulted in clashes between the different communities, then under UN intervention. France sent an aircraft carrier to the Adriatic, as part of Task Force (TF) 470, ready to support the UNPROFOR (UN Protection Force) and then the IFOR (Implementation Force). SUEs, followed by SEMs, were on the go for several years, alternating embarkations on *Clemenceau* and *Foch* from January 1993 onward. During Operation *Balbuzard III* in September 1993, 11F, still equipped with the SUE, attacked targets in Bosnia with unguided bombs. In the meantime, from April 1993 until December 1995, Operation *Deny Flight* was launched. *Foch* and *Clemenceau* followed one another once again in the Adriatic, with about 15 Super Étendards on board. Between August and September 1995, Operation *Deliberate Force* covered an intense bombing campaign aimed against the Serbs. The Super Étendards carried out a few war missions and intervened with unguided bombs, but their attack calculator remained poorly suited to bombing operations from medium altitude (imposed by the AAA threat), and the lack of precision was felt.

From December 1995 to December 1996, operations *Salamander I, II* and *III* followed one another, with the surveillance of Bosnian airspace and strikes against Bosnian Serb militias.

In the meantime, the Balkans ignited again, and Europe learned of new irredentist demands, this time in Kosovo. TF 470 set sail again in January 1999, with 11F's Standard 3 SEMs on board along with the first laser-guided GBU-12s. The SEMs were kept on alert on *Foch*, ready to support the French forces stationed in Macedonia. From March to June 1999, NATO led Operation *Allied Force* against Serbia. On 30 March 1999, the SEMs were catapulted with GBU-12s for their first attack mission against Serbian targets. However, the bad weather above their targets prevented them from firing and the pilots were forced to drop their ammunition in the sea before landing back on the carrier.

The first bombs actually fired against their objectives were discharged on 5 April. The carrier air group, which included up to 16 SEMs, then carried out an average of 14 offensive sorties per day to provide close air support (CAS) or 'Battlefield Air Interdiction' deep in Serbian territory, more than 400km from *Foch*.

The missions followed one another throughout the month of April, without loss but with varying success depending on the weather conditions; bad weather considerably hindered the acquisition and

Right: Crew members carried the catapult bridle to a Super Étendard armed with an AS30L missile. (Marine nationale)

identification of targets using the laser designation pods. The SEM then used the ATLIS II nacelle, also in service on the Mirage 2000D, which meant only daytime missions were possible. The aircraft flew in pairs, one acting as an illuminator and the other one as a shooter, carrying two 250kg GBU-12s. Barracuda dual-band jammers and Phimat flare launchers were systematically fitted. In May 1999, Standard 3 SEMs were finally allowed to land back on the carrier with their bombs. It was about time; before that date, 49 bombs had to be dropped into the sea when they could not be launched against the targets! Initially, however, the aircraft remained limited to 20 deck landings each with the GBU-12s in order not to exceed the wear limit on the airframes.

Above: An AS30L waiting to be installed under the wing of a SEM. The missile's wings were not in place yet. (Marine nationale)

Left: The GBU-12's markings, as seen on a SEM during Operation *Allied Force*. (Frédéric Lert)

Between 26 January and 3 June 1999, the SEMs carried out 1,800 flight hours in 412 bombing missions (240 CAS missions and 172 Battlefield Air Interdictions) and 245 in-flight refuellings. The SEMs dropped a total of 268 munitions, including the 49 GBU-12s dumped in the sea and two AS30L missiles fired against munitions depots at the Serbian airfield in Ponikve. No free-fall bombs were launched by the SEMs during this conflict and the French Navy's score was said to be one of the best in NATO, with 78 per cent of the bombs on target.

Right: On *Foch*, GBU-12s were brought on the deck via the aircraft elevator. (Marine nationale)

Below: SEM No 13 cleared the deck with an AS30L under its right wing. (Marine nationale)

Afghanistan: the unlikely adventure

The SEMs were on board nuclear aircraft carrier *Charles de Gaulle* when it was engaged in Operation *Héraclès* (the French counterpart of Operation *Enduring Freedom*) from 1 December 2001, three months after the 9/11 attacks. From 17F, 16 aircraft were embarked on the aircraft carrier, half of them Standard 3 and the other half Standard 4. Operational flights over Afghanistan began on 19 December.

The French aircraft, which only had the ATLIS II pod, were once again confined to daytime missions. In just over 2,000 flight hours, only 13 250kg BLU-111s were dropped, but much of the activity was devoted to photo reconnaissance with the CRM 280 chassis. *Charles de Gaulle* returned to Toulon on 1 July 2002, after seven months at sea.

SEM No 45 was ready to strike hard with two GBU-12s underwing. The wingman who took the picture carried the laser designation pod. (Marine nationale)

It took three aircraft to drop two laser-guided ammunitions. The SEM was a small aircraft with a limited payload indeed! (ARDHAN)

During their first operational deployment, the Rafale Ms had limited air-to-ground capabilities and the aircraft were mainly used for support missions, such as 'buddy-buddy' refuelling. (Benjamin Vinot Prefontaine)

'Buddy-buddy' refuelling was a common procedure for the Super Étendard. (Benjamin Vinot Prefontaine)

Tanking on the US Air Force KC-10. The two-toned camouflage of this SEM signified that the aircraft was coming from *Charles de Gaulle* and not from Kandahar. (Benjamin Vinot Prefontaine)

The SEM had no problem tanking with Boeings, provided they were fitted with the wing pods and flexible hoses. (Benjamin Vinot Prefontaine)

Formation flying on a French E-2C Hawkeye. On some occasions, the E-2C went deep into Afghan territory to act as a control and command aircraft when an AWACS was not available. (Benjamin Vinot Prefontaine)

The Rafale M dropped its first bomb in Afghanistan on 28 March 2007. A SEM provided the laser target designation. (Benjamin Vinot Prefontaine)

Tanking on a French Air Force C-135FR. The wing pods enabled two aircraft to be refuelled at the same time. (Benjamin Vinot Prefontaine)

Here, high above the Kandahar NATO Air Force Base, SEM No 1 was flying with two GBU-49 GPS-guided bombs under the left wing and the Damocles pod in the centerline under the fuselage. (Frédéric Lert collection)

In April 2004, a brief passage of *Charles de Gaulle* off the Pakistani coast gave the SEMs an opportunity to accumulate a few additional missions over Afghanistan. The manoeuvre was repeated in 2006, again with very few bombings. At the end of 2006, the first Standard 5 aircraft arrived in the flottille. These aircraft were equipped with the Damocles nacelle (which had entered service the previous year on the Standard 4), which could be used day and night for laser illumination, laser pointer, laser spot tracking, Flir and more.

In March 2007, *Charles de Gaulle* was again back off the coast of Pakistan for a new episode of the *Héraclès* mission. The deployment was marked by the first air-to-ground combat fire of the French Navy's Rafale M, with the SEMs providing the target's laser designation with their Damocles pods.

The highlight of the SEM's intervention in Afghanistan came in the summer of 2008, with the deployment of three aircraft to Kandahar Air Base. The SEM was not the aircraft best suited for operations conducted in the heart of the Afghan summer, with its infernal temperatures and a terrain 3,500ft (more than 1,000m) above sea level. Luckily enough, Kandahar's runway was a long one, with 3,200m available.

In Kandahar, when their performance allowed, the aircraft took off in a two bombs configuration, with two GBUs under the left wing and a 1,100-litre external tank under the right one. However, most of the time, the SEM's lack of power only allowed it to carry a single 250kg bomb, counterbalanced by a 600-litre tank. The Navy had also taken CRM 280 reconnaissance chassis to Kandahar, but these were not used. On the other hand, the SEMs fighting in Afghanistan were at their best technically, with two trump cards: the Fightacs tactical pad and the GBU-49 bomb. The first copies of the Fightacs pads were supplied by the manufacturer (EADS) in the spring of 2008, just in time to participate in the Kandahar detachment. This lightweight pad allowed the pilot to consult all kinds of documents, like maps and photographs. It was associated with a computer, the size of a laptop, positioned behind the ejection seat, that served as an interface with the various on-board systems. The integration of the GBU-49 with GPS/laser guidance on the SEM was, for its part, a real achievement for the aircraft, which was the first one to have this dual guidance capability in France. The first bombs were dropped in France on a training range two months before departure for Afghanistan, and each Landivisiau-based pilot earmarked for the Afghan deployment had the opportunity to fire one.

As one pilot recalled:

We were off the performance charts we had for the aircraft. A hot weather campaign had taken place in the 1980s in Djibouti [northeast Africa], but the performance curves were not drawn above 35°C. In Kandahar, the SEM suffered from the altitude, the heat and its lack of power. We were taking off with the flaps retracted to gain speed on the runway more quickly. But the acceleration was very long, so that we had a 'dead zone' between 100kt and the 150kt necessary for the take-off: we knew that we did not have enough room to stop in case of a problem between these two speeds.

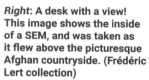

Right: **A desk with a view! This image shows the inside of a SEM, and was taken as it flew above the picturesque Afghan countryside. (Frédéric Lert collection)**

Below: **The Super Étendard Modernisé Standard 5, an example of which is seen here, was able to 'lase' the targets for its own bombs. (Frédéric Lert collection)**

An aircraft on take-off from Kandahar, with the highly distinctive former commercial terminal in the background. (YF)

SEM No 24 under a shelter before a dawn mission from Kandahar Air Force Base. (Baron)

Six aircraft and 15 pilots, therefore, took turns in Kandahar in two detachments. The first one, led by 17F, took over from three Armée de l'air Rafales from the 1/7 Provence Squadron at the beginning of June 2008. After 88 sorties, representing 387 flight hours, these first aircraft were replaced by those of the second detachment, which arrived in Afghanistan on 27 July. The Navy aircraft left the country for good in October 2008. They were replaced with three Armée de l'air Mirage 2000Ds.

Between the first operational mission on 6 June 2008 and their departure on 5 October, the French Navy pilots accumulated 930 flight hours and 244 sorties from Kandahar. About 20 bombs were fired (the first drop took place on 7 June 2008), with 100 per cent on target.

Operation *Harmattan* in Libya

Operation *Harmattan* was the name given to the French intervention in Libya, which began on 19 March 2011. On 20 March, the carrier task force centred on *Charles de Gaulle* left Toulon, the main French naval base on the Mediterranean shore. On the aircraft carrier's deck was an air group made up of ten Rafale Ms, six SEMs, two Grumman Hawkeye E-2Cs and five helicopters.

Because Operation *Harmattan* was launched shortly after the return of *Charles de Gaulle* from the *Agapanthe* training mission, which had seen the engagement of 13 SEMs, the aircraft had been in high demand, and many aircraft were undergoing technical regeneration at the start of operations in Libya. Rafales and SEMs continued to fly and fight together for the reasons explained by the 17F commander at the time: 'At the very beginning of *Harmattan*, joint patrols made it possible to compensate for the insufficient number of Damocles pods, or even Rafale pilots qualified for their use. These patrols were very effective, as they put together

During Operation *Harmattan* against Libya, SEMs, Rafale Ms and E-2C Hawkeyes shared *Charles de Gaulle*'s deck. (Marine nationale)

An armourer loaded the flare dispensers that were hooked under the so-called 'point zero' hard point. These dispensers came with the SEM Standard 4. (Frédéric Lert)

Ready to shoot the catapult! This SEM carried two flare dispensers under its wings, between the fuselage and the external fuel tanks. (Marine nationale)

A few weeks after Operation *Harmattan* ended in March 2011, the French Navy showcased its best tools, such as the SEM with two GBU-49s under the right wing. (Frédéric Lert)

The six SEMs that had been based in Kandahar from June 2008 had previously received a new integral grey camouflage, which they kept when they flew back to France. (Frédéric Lert)

SEM pilots experienced in the use of the pod and the Rafale which could carry up to six bombs simultaneously.'

The carrier air group then only had six SEMs, served by around 15 pilots, coming initially from 17F. After a few weeks of operation, 11F pilots started to take over from them. By the end of *Harmattan*, virtually all SEM pilots had experienced the fighting over Libya.

Tasked against targets on land, the carrier air group also participated in the destruction of the Libyan Navy. The aim was to destroy all operational Libyan vessels at once and to avoid any reaction on their part. Ships had to be attacked in ports and three were targeted: Tripoli to the west, Sirte to the east and Al Khums in between. Combattant II missile patrol boats were present in each port, and the frigate *Al Girdabiyah* (Koni type) was anchored in Tripoli.

The strikes had to be carried out at night, with a Grumman Hawkeye taking charge of the coordination. To the great regret of the French Navy pilots, the attack had to be carried out with bombs and not with the Exocet missile. Two SEMs were entrusted with the attack on Sirte; the first aircraft was equipped with the Damocles pod and two 1,100-litre external fuel tanks, and the second one carried two 125kg GBU-58s with three 600-litre fuel tanks. Despite these very different configurations, the two aircraft ended up with practically the same quantity of fuel (4,300 litres for the leader and 4,000 litres for the wingman) and, therefore, an identical 'playtime'. The attack on Al Khums was given to the Royal Air Force, while Tripoli received the visit from two Mirage 2000Ds from the Armée de l'air and two Rafale Ms from the French Navy.

A pilot who took part in the mission told the story:

We were launched around 10pm. Immediately after leaving the carrier, we took about 800kg of fuel on the 'nounou', which gave us a playtime of about 90 minutes, with the carrier not far from the coast. It was a very comfortable situation to drop two bombs [...] But in Sirte, the weather was not so good, with a thin cloud layer over the harbour, and we orbited for thirty minutes, waiting for the clouds to disperse. The other patrols were also waiting for our 'go' to shoot. We took advantage of this half hour to find the best solution for the attack and make a few rehearsal bombing runs. At night we weren't bothered by the sun and there was little wind, the only constraint came from the clouds

Operation *Harmattan* once again demonstrated the operational flexibility of the SEM and its 30 or so weapon configurations. In the early days, faced with a credible threat (air-to-air and surface-to-air), the aircraft carried a self-protection Magic missile, a Barracuda jamming pod with one or two bombs, and an additional fuel tank under the fuselage. The missile and the jammer were subsequently removed, freeing up space for additional fuel tanks under the wing.

Flying Air Interdiction missions, the SEM could carry four GBU-49s hung two by two under the AUF2 launchers, with a 600-litre fuel tank under the fuselage. It was a convenient configuration used for the first time during the operation on missions that did not require a significant playtime, as the GPS-guided ammunitions were programmed before the launch. The SEMs also fired around ten AS30L missiles during Operation *Harmattan*, a perfect attack against bunkers and hardened shelters.

Operation *Chammal*: the SEM's last stand

In the early days of 2015, aircraft carrier *Charles de Gaulle* set sail for the Indian Ocean for the first *Arromanches* mission. After some joint training with different air forces in the eastern Mediterranean, the ship joined American Task Force 50 in the Persian Gulf. In coordination with aircraft carrier *Carl Vinson*, *Charles de Gaulle* participated for eight weeks in Operation *Chammal*, the French operation against the Islamic State in Iraq and Syria. The aircraft carrier and its air group then returned to France on 19 May 2015. After a few weeks of rest, a second *Arromanches* mission was launched at the end of 2015. On 18 November, the carrier strike group set sail once more for the eastern Mediterranean. On board *Charles de Gaulle*, the air group was made up of 18 Rafale Ms, eight SEMs, two Hawkeyes and three helicopters.

For its last operational embarkation, the SEM had two advantages up its sleeve: the GBU-49 guided bomb and the use of the last ATLIS pods, which was still in operation and still in the race for daytime operations. The day and night Damocles pod, the only one usable by the Rafale M, was not always available in sufficient numbers, so the ATLIS offered an interesting alternative.

'For its last use in combat, the SEM certainly showed its age, but it represented a remarkable effort to optimize its capabilities', explained Lieutenant Commander V, then commander of 17F. 'We used several configurations, starting with the one combining the ATLIS pod and two fuel tanks and two 125kg GBU-58s under the wings. We also carried the 5081 Alkan flare launchers mixing IR and EM cartridges. Considering a two-aircraft strike, if the first one was equipped with GBU-58s, the other could carry one or two GBU-49s. The GBU-12s were not used in Syria, the '49' doing the job just as well with the added flexibility provided by GPS guidance'. During *Arromanches*, the French Navy chose to abandon mixed patrols with Rafale M. 'It was easier to manage missions with identical aircraft, with the same flight profiles, the same speeds, the same playtime in the area and above all identical access to the tankers', stated Lieutenant Commander V.

From the maintenance point of view, the last SEM engagement in the *Arromanches 2* mission was also a success. The former Chief of Technical Services of 17F explained:

We started 2015 with eleven operational aircraft, of which three, numbers 8, 10 and 12, were reaching the end of their life. These three aircraft were mainly used for pilot training in Landivisiau, knowing that they would not offer enough flying hours for an overseas mission. In October 2015, number 8 reached the end of its life and was transferred to Rochefort's maintenance school. And aircraft 10 and 12 remained at Landivisiau when the *Arromanches 2* mission was launched in early November. *Charles de Gaulle* therefore embarked the last eight aircraft, whose potentials had been carefully managed to face this last tasking.

These eight aircraft took part in the bulk of the operation, with the oldest, Nos 19, 43 and 46, finally leaving the party in mid-March 2016, having reached their potential limit. Flottille 17F then finished this last operation on SEMs, with the last five aircraft. 'The availability of the aircraft was excellent until the end', recalled the Chief, 'we had all the necessary spares and know-how, and we were particularly at ease.'

On 16 March 2016, the last SEMs on board the aircraft carrier returning from the Middle East were launched towards the shore under a low and humid sky. Two of these aircraft flew to Hyères, where they ended their careers in the hands of young sailors training to become aircraft handlers on the carrier.

The others, each still having 100 or so hours of potential, took off for Landivisiau where they served during the last weeks of their working life to train young pilots. On 12 July 2016, everything stopped definitively, with the SEMs withdrawn from service during an official ceremony at the Landivisiau Naval Base.

No doubt the French Navy lost a great soldier with the SEM – a 'Swiss Army Knife', as the pilots used to say. The SEM was an aircraft with no afterburner, no optronics or multifunction displays, but the aircraft was perfectly sized for small 30,000 tonnes aircraft carriers and benefited throughout its career from well-thought-out investments to keep it level.

'At one point, I searched the world to see if an aircraft offered such a wide range of missions and I couldn't find one', said a former flottille commander. The F-15 or the F-16? They were not equipped to do buddy-buddy aerial refuelling. The F/A-18? It was not equipped with a nuclear-strike missile. The SEM had it all.

Chapter 5

The Super Étendards of the Antipodes

I n July 1979, the Argentinian junta ordered 14 Super Étendards to equip the 2a Escuadrilla Aeronaval de Caza y Ataque in Puerto Belgrano. This unit had to be able to embark on aircraft carrier *25 de Mayo*, which was being retrofitted to precisely accommodate the French aircraft. In April 1981, an Argentine delegation of ten pilots, all with prior Skyhawk experience, and 20 mechanics arrived in Landivisiau to learn the new aircraft.

Ramon Josa, a French SUE pilot of Spanish origin, who played a key role in the contract with Argentina, remembered:

It was contractually agreed that each pilot would fly 50 hours in France, not a minute more. It was further agreed that we would only train Argentines to fly the aircraft and to use the navigation and weapon system, the head-up display, the inertial system, etc. There was no question of training in tactics. That said, all pilots were experienced men, with prior knowledge of carrier operations and they were delighted with the aircraft, just as we were. They were very competent, and we were very far with them from the difficulties that we would experience later with the Iraqis.

When all the pilots completed their 50-hour flight time, they all returned to Argentina, apart from two who stayed in France to train for a Landing Signal Officer (LSO) qualification. The other pilots did not have the opportunity to fly simulated deck landings, let alone board the French aircraft carriers. However, the two future LSOs had to qualify on the carrier, and they each logged six landings and as many catapultings on *Foch*.

Only five aircraft and five Exocet missiles were delivered before the embargo caused by the invasion of the Falklands. These modest figures were enough to exact a heavy toll on the Royal Navy. It remained somewhat of a mystery why Argentina did not wait until it received its full complement of aircraft and missiles (14 aircraft and a first batch of 20 missiles were ordered) before engaging in its stand-off with Britain.

Four missions were launched by the Argentines against the British fleet during the Falklands War. The priority targets were the aircraft carriers HMS *Invincible* and HMS *Hermes*, whose Sea Harriers were a major hindrance to the Argentine Air Force. Even before firing a single missile, the presence of the Super Étendard had a beneficial effect for the Argentines, as it forced the British to position their naval forces far east of the Falklands to keep them away from the threat. In doing so, the British diminished their ability to strike on land.

The first Exocet mission took place on 4 May 1982 and involved two SUEs, discreetly informed about the position of the British fleet by a maritime patrol P-2H Neptune. The objectives were located more than 600km from the Super Étendard launch base in Tierra del Fuego. Such a distance implied an in-flight refuelling en route, which was carried out by a KC-130H. After the refuelling, the fighters 'hit the deck' and charged in the estimated direction of the British fleet, in very bad weather conditions. One hour and 20 minutes after take-off, the two aircraft each fired an Exocet against the nearest target.

HMS *Sheffield* was hit by a missile and had to be abandoned by its crew after three hours of fighting against the flames. The second missile was certainly deceived.

The next day, 23 May, a new mission was launched, but the aircraft returned to their base without being able to fire. On 25 May, another ambitious attack was launched. A group of British ships was spotted 800km from the Argentinian coast. The mission again involved two aircraft, lasted four hours and required two in-flight refuellings. The Argentinian pilots fired their two missiles against a strong radar echo, hoping it was an aircraft carrier. It was, in fact, a container ship, *Atlantic Conveyor*, the loss of which led to the destruction of the ten helicopters it was carrying in its hold. A final attack was attempted on 30 May against the British aircraft carriers with the last missile available to the Argentines. The Argentinian pilots claimed on their return that an aircraft carrier had been hit and that it was HMS *Invincible*. The British denied that one of their aircraft carriers has been hit by an Exocet. Three decades later, doubt still hangs over this episode, and a possible scenario could have been a near miss, with an explosion slightly damaging the ship, but with no direct hit.

There is no doubt that, had the Argentine forces received the 20 missiles ordered, the toll would have been much heavier for the Royal Navy. When asked if the French Navy would have done better than the Argentines when faced with an identical scenario, the answer from Ramon Josa was unequivocally: 'Probably not!'

With the Falklands War over, Argentina received the last nine Super Étendards in November 1982. On 18 April 1983, an Argentinian SUE made contact for the first time with the deck of Argentinian aircraft carrier *25 de Mayo*.

An Argentinian Super Étendard performing a touch-and-go on USS *Ronald Reagan* in June 2004. (US Navy)

On 4 May 1982, the Argentine Navy's Super Étendard launched the two Exocets that would ultimately sink HMS *Sheffield*. **This painting is from talented French artist Daniel Bechennec. (MBDA)**

Since 1993, Argentine pilots have practised their skill on board the neighbouring Brazilian Navy's aircraft carrier *Sao Paulo* (ex-*Foch*). Touch-and-go landing exercises have been common also on US Navy carriers during joint exercises. In 2017, five Super Étendard Modernisés (the aircraft was already phased out in France) along with a simulator, eight spare engines, and a large batch of spares and tooling were purchased from France to bolster the fleet at a cost of €12.5 million.

Operation *Milan*: when the Super Étendard fought for Saddam Hussein

In 1983, Iraq wanted to block Iranian maritime traffic in the Persian Gulf and asked France to supply five Super Étendards armed with AM39 Exocet missiles. This was to be an interim measure, pending delivery of the Mirage F1 EQ5, a highly capable Mirage F1 version (including for anti-shipping missions with the Exocet) that Iraq had also ordered from France. Paris accepted Baghdad's request, but with the production line of the Super Étendard terminated, the aircraft had to be borrowed from the French Navy. Five aircraft (SUE Nos 65, 66, 67, 68 and 69) just off the production line were thus sold, with the promise to buy them back after a few months of use. In order to comply with the Iraqi request, France decided to organise and launch a secret leasing operations, codenamed *Milan*. However, before sending them to the Middle East, the Iraqis had to be trained, and it was quite an adventure.

Six pilots and 40 mechanics were sent to Landivisiau. All of them had a previous experience on combat aircraft but, to quote a French instructor who worked with them, 'five were very bad and the sixth was very good'.

Above and below: Training the Iraqi pilots over the French countryside in 1983. All the codes and national markings were removed from the aircraft. (ARDHAN)

SUE No 65 was one of the five aircraft 'sold' to Iraq. It was later given back to the French Navy. (ARDHAN)

After three months of extreme emotions, the six pilots each completed about 60 hours of flight. However, the ferrying of the aircraft (whose avionics had been partially modified) to Iraq was entrusted to French pilots. The SUEs left Landivisiau on 7 October 1983, heading for Mesopotamia, with a pit stop on a French carrier in the middle of the Mediterranean Sea. The first operational missions were launched toward the Iranian oil terminal at Kharg from March 1984.

According to information published in the French media by a former French technical assistant, the Iraqis carried out 175 operational missions between March 1984 and March 1985. Between 70 and 75 Exocet missiles were fired and around 60 ships hit. Three or four missiles failed, and the remaining ten went to strike decoys. SUE No 67 was lost on 16 September 1984, when it struck the sea during a low-level flight. The other four aircraft were returned to France after just over a year of use. They were in very good condition, having flown little (about ten hours per month at most) and having benefited from a very dry climate.

Apart from Argentina and Iraq, the Super Étendard was unsuccessful in the export market. The Mirage F1 quickly replaced the aircraft on the final assembly line in Mérignac, and the very sophisticated Mirage F1 EQ5 took over the anti-shipping missions with Iraqi pilots. Interestingly enough, during the Paris Air Show in 1987, Dassault Aviation displayed Super Étendard No 37 with a desert camouflage in a bid to find new export customers. As No 37 was known to have some cracks in its structure, it was limited to a +2g acceleration and was not presented in flight. The move was rather bizarre, as production of the Super Étendard had ceased five years earlier, and, logically, no customers showed interest. Thus, the commercial career of the aircraft ended for good.

FURTHER READING FROM

As Europe's leading transport publisher, we also produce a range of market-leading aviation magazines and specials.